THROUGH
LOSS INTO
LIGHT

A JOURNEY OF GRIEF, HEALING,
AND THE LOVE THAT REMAINS

Lisa Thompson, PhD

ISBN: 979-8-9992030-9-0

Book Design by Transcendent Publishing
Author Portrait by Ilana Maxwell
Edited by Mary Rembert

Some names and identifying details have been changed to protect individuals' privacy. Events, locations, and conversations have been recreated from memory, and in certain instances, names, identifying characteristics, occupations, and places of residence have been altered to maintain anonymity.

Printed in the United States of America.

"Grief is like the ocean; it comes in waves, ebbing and flowing. Sometimes the water is calm, and sometimes it is overwhelming. All we can do is learn to swim."

–Vicki Harrison

CONTENTS

DEDICATION

For Skip

Thank you for loving me in this lifetime with a depth that healed something ancient. Your departure reshaped everything, and in the space it left behind, I found the truth of who I am.

You were the catalyst. You helped me remember.

And for every soul who has loved and lost, who has questioned everything and still kept walking, may these pages hold your hand through the dark and remind you that love never leaves. It only changes form.

ACKNOWLEDGMENTS

I am eternally grateful for my late husband, Skip. His love shaped me, and his departure changed me. He's continued to guide me in ways both subtle and profound through dreams, synchronicities, and soul nudges. I am thankful for all the ways he still walks beside me, his presence that never truly left, and the strength he lends me as I carry this work forward.

To my children, Mila and Curran, thank you for your patience and your love during a time when I didn't have all the answers. I know it wasn't easy, and I hope you always feel how deeply I honor the ways you each moved through your own loss. You continue to teach me what it means to love with presence. I hope you always know how proud I am to be your mother. Please know and trust that Skip loved you greatly, and he is still watching over you.

To Jen, you've been my constant, my friend, my rock, and my soul mate. You have witnessed every stage of this transformation without ever needing me to be anything other than exactly who I am. Thank you for your devotion, your humor, your fierce love, and your steady presence through the fires of loss and the beauty of becoming.

To my friend and mentor Sunny, I cannot thank you enough for your clarity, compassion, and realness. You were a lighthouse for me in my darkest moments. Your generosity and insights were more appreciated than words can express.

To Jodie, I want to thank you for checking in on me daily during those first few months. Your intuition, kindness, and ability to hold space made it easier for me to trust my own unfolding.

To the women of the Galactic Retreat, you came into my life at such a potent moment. Thank you for trusting me to guide you, and for reflecting back the very healing I was moving through myself. The space we shared was sacred, and your presence helped anchor something new in me. The retreat took a very different turn than we had anticipated, and I honor your willingness to pivot.

To Isaiah, I want to thank you for showing up in my life when I was rediscovering who I was. You came into my life like a soul memory I couldn't ignore. Thank you for the sanctuary we created, for the way you helped me reclaim beauty and life in the very place where I had lost so much. Our connection shaped this book in ways you may never fully realize. I will always love you.

And to you, dear reader, thank you for meeting me here and walking with me through this story. I hope something in these pages reminds you that healing is possible, love is eternal, and we're never walking alone.

INTRODUCTION

I never thought this would be the book I'd be writing. Not now, and definitely not like this.

When Skip died, everything fell apart. One moment, we were living our lives, messy and imperfect, but full of love. The next, he was gone, and I was standing in the middle of a reality I couldn't explain. I was trying to make sense of something that didn't make sense.

I had already written a book about us, *Sacred Soul Love*. I thought that was it, that was our story. The meeting, the healing, and the conscious partnership. I thought we were just getting started.

This is the part of the story I never expected to tell. This is what came after.

Skip was one of the most loving, goofy, big-hearted humans I've ever known. He made people laugh. He gave the best hugs. He wasn't perfect, of course, but he loved with everything he had. Life with him had its challenging moments. It also had beautiful experiences and adventures. It was never dull. I always knew I was loved.

This book isn't just about grief. It's about what gets uncovered when everything falls apart. It's about who you become when everything familiar disappears. It's about listening to what's still here when the person you love is no longer in a body.

After Skip passed, things got weird. Time got stretchy. Messages started coming in from him, from spirit, and from parts of me I hadn't fully remembered. Galactic energy returned in ways I couldn't ignore. Underneath all of it, I kept hearing the same thing: Come home to yourself, even in the pain and the not-knowing. Especially there.

Some of what I'll share is raw. Some of it's mystical. Some of it might sound a little out there. Some of it is just me, sitting on the bedroom floor, trying to remember how to keep breathing.

This isn't a how-to or a five-step process for healing, awakening, or moving on. It's a real story of my own understanding of life after death and how I moved through grief.

If you've ever had your heart ripped open by someone leaving, whether by choice or by force, or if you've ever found yourself in the ashes of a life you thought you were building … this is for you.

I don't have it all figured out, but I keep walking. Maybe something I share here will help you to keep walking too.

FROM MY HEART TO YOURS

Even when everything breaks, you're not broken. Even when you can't see the path, you're still on it. There's no right way to grieve, no clean arc to healing, but there is a way through.

And there is always love, not just in what was or in what's coming, but in who you are now.

To walk through grief is to walk through a threshold, one that asks more of you than you might think you can give. My life's work is devoted to helping people move through grief, awaken to the love that still surrounds them, and find healing in places they never thought possible.

That's why I created something to support you as you keep going. It's a free gift from my heart to yours, designed to help you connect with your loved one beyond the veil and deepen your relationship with them in the unseen realms.

If the words in this book have stirred something in you—an ache, a spark, a quiet remembering, this gift is here to help you go further. It's not about having the answers. It's about feeling the love that never left. You can receive it here:

TheLoveThatRemains.com

SECTION 1

Walking Through Love, Loss, and the Call of Purpose

"Grief is the last act of love we can give to those we loved. Where there is deep grief, there was great love."

–Anonymous

CHAPTER 1

THE VOWS WE MADE

We got married on the rooftop of our hotel in Phuket, Thailand. It was December 22, 2018. The sun was high in the sky, casting warm tropical light over the ocean. The only person present with us was our Thai tour guide, who graciously agreed to be our witness and photographer.

It was perfect and straightforward. There was no grand ceremony, no rows of guests or elaborate plans. It was just the two of us, standing in the midday heat, surrounded by sky and sea, promising our lives to each other, and sweating our asses off.

And honestly, that was so us … Skip didn't need pomp or attention. What mattered to him was the feeling, the truth of it. He loved the freedom of being somewhere beautiful, away from the world's expectations, doing things in our own way. That rooftop became our temple, with the ocean as our choir.

I looked into his eyes that day and saw everything I had always hoped for in a partner. Skip was goofy and affectionate. He always made me laugh when I took life too seriously. He was loyal, steady, and supportive. He was the kind of man who truly showed up, not just when it was easy, but especially when it was hard. He loved with his whole being. When he held me, it felt like home.

We spoke our vows from the heart through words we had written to each other. They weren't long, but they were sacred. We promised to love each other fully, to support one another's dreams, to honor each other's growth, and to keep choosing each other, even when life got messy.

I didn't know then how short our time would be or how deeply those vows would echo after he was gone. I did know, in every cell of my being, that our connection was more than Earth-deep. Skip wasn't just my husband. He was my soul companion. I could feel the threads between us stretching far beyond this lifetime, into something older and more expansive than I could explain at the time.

There were moments with him that felt like déjà vu in the most profound sense, like we had loved each other before, in different bodies, and on different timelines. Even now, after his passing, I can still feel him. The bond didn't break. It just changed form.

In my previous book, *Sacred Soul Love*, I shared how we found each other after heartbreak and how we created a life of deep love, presence, and play. But what I hadn't written, because I hadn't lived it yet, was what happens when that kind of love remains after the person is gone. What does it become? How does it transform you?

This chapter of our story is the one where we said *yes* to each other, our soul contract, and to the journey ahead, including the parts we couldn't yet see. Even with all the pain that came later, I would still go back and do it all over again. I would still say yes, because loving Skip was one of the greatest honors of my life. The vows we made are still alive in me, guiding what comes next.

Our Wedding Vows

Skip's Vows to Me:

I, Steven Karl Thompson, choose you, Lisa, to be my wife. I accept you as you are, and I offer myself in return.

I choose you because you complete me. You allow me to be myself and love me for it.

I choose you because when I am with you, I breathe deeper and feel love throughout my body.

I choose you because when I hold you, I feel your immense energy and love.

I choose you because I feel like we have been together in other lives and were meant to be reunited for this life and others to come.

I vow:

To take you as you are, loving who you are now and who you will become.

To listen to you and learn from you, to support you and accept your support.

To be joy to your heart and food for your soul.

To learn with you and grow with you, even as time and life change us both.

To love you, encourage you, and trust you in all aspects of our lives.

To respect you as a person, a business professional, a partner, a mother, and all the roles we will play in each other's lives.

To love you just as much on a sunny day as on a rainy day.

To love you when things are perfect and when life presents challenges.

To share my victories and defeats with you and celebrate your triumphs and mourn your losses as though they were my own.

To laugh with you in times of joy and comfort you in times of sorrow.

To share in your dreams and support you as you strive to achieve your goals.

To listen to you with compassion and understanding and speak to you with encouragement.

To love you and have faith in your love for me, through all our years and all that life may bring us.

Today, I marry you with no hesitation or doubt, and my commitment to you is absolute. I promise to choose you every day, to love you in word and deed, and to do the hard work in making *now* into *always*.

Will you marry me and share your life with me?

My Vows to Skip:

Skip, you are truly the love of my life, not just this one life, but so many others before this.

When I first met you, I felt an instant connection. I knew there was something special about you, and I just had to be around you as much as possible.

I will never forget our first date when we went dancing with Tracie and Jeff. I couldn't stop smiling and giggling, and I still can't. The day we spent in Seattle on the longest date ever showed me that our relationship was meant to be. And then I got to learn patience and trust as you were healing.

The last three and a half years with you have been the best years of my life. I love our adventures together. I love the respect and admiration we have for each other. I love how you make me a better person in so many ways. You continually inspire me.

You are my person. I love you more than I ever knew could be possible. You balance me out perfectly, and you fit into my family, now our family, like the missing puzzle piece.

My promise to you is that I will love and respect you every day of our lives. You are my best friend and confidante. You are my life partner.

I look forward to spending the rest of my life with you, exploring the world as well as each other. I want to wake up each day in your arms and hold your hand throughout this journey of life together.

I am your mirror, and you are mine. I want you to see how loved you are when you look into my eyes. I want you to feel my love when I touch you. I want you to know without a doubt that your heart is safe with me.

I commit my heart and soul to you in this life and beyond. I am honored to be your wife, your queen, your goddess.

I marry you today, knowing the universe brought us together and that our life moving forward flows with ease, joy, and endless love.

Please take this ring and wear it as a token and reminder of my love and commitment to you.

I love you.

CHAPTER 2

ADVENTURES WITH SKIP

Before the grief and the unraveling, there was laughter. One of the best parts about being with Skip was how fun life became. He had this light in him that didn't just brighten rooms; it softened them.

His goofiness wasn't performative; it came from a place of pure, unfiltered joy. Whether we were road-tripping, snorkeling, hiking, or just making coffee together in the morning, he brought a playfulness to everything we did.

Adventure was part of our rhythm from the start. We explored new places together, not just to check them off a list, but to experience them, and to live in them. Skip had this way of noticing the small things— quirky signs, street food smells, and how the light hit the waves. He found beauty in them.

One of our most unforgettable trips was to Cancun, Mexico, in 2017. I had been a shark biologist earlier in my life, so my love for marine life ran deep. From the very beginning of our relationship, I knew that Skip was deathly afraid of sharks. It wasn't subtle. It was a deep, visceral fear. So when I told him I wanted to swim with whale sharks, I knew exactly what I was asking of him. And still, he did it. He got on the boat, suited up, and got in the water for me.

As he immersed himself in the open ocean surrounded by these majestic, gentle giants, his heart was pounding the whole time, but he never made it about him. He let it be about us.

His courage that day didn't just touch me. It changed me. It also changed him. There's a unique kind of love that shows up in the face of fear. That's what Skip gave me.

Another powerful memory came from our trip to Belize in 2019. It was part adventure and part heart-opening immersion. We explored ancient Mayan ruins, climbing temple steps that overlooked the jungle, and feeling the weight of history in the stone beneath our hands.

Skip was fascinated. We stood at the top of one of the temples together, gazing out at the canopy of trees below, not saying much, but completely present. There was a stillness there. A reverence.

Then, in classic Skip-and-Lisa fashion, we followed that sacred experience with an adrenaline rush, a visit to Shark Alley. The boat guide chummed the water, and within minutes, numerous nurse sharks swarmed around us, accompanied by a few gliding stingrays.

The water churned, alive with motion. Skip, terrified but brave, stayed in the water with the sharks. I watched him summon the same courage I'd seen in Cancun. He faced his fear, held my hand, and swam through it anyway.

Not all our travels were easy. One trip in particular almost broke us. In the spring of 2018, we went to Sedona, Arizona. I brought my two kids, Mila and Curran, and we hoped for a restorative, family-bonding trip in the red rocks.

Almost from the start, the energy felt strained. Tensions surfaced between parenting styles, communication patterns, and unspoken stressors. Emotions ran high, and by the third day, everything felt fragile.

Sedona has a way of stripping illusions and showing you what's underneath. One evening, we decided to go on a UFO night tour. I wasn't expecting anything life-changing, but something happened when I looked through those military-grade night vision goggles at the vast Arizona sky. I saw things moving, lightships, patterns, and intelligence that I hadn't witnessed for many years. Something clicked inside me, and a long-forgotten part of myself stirred. I couldn't unsee it.

That night planted a seed that wouldn't bloom until a few years later, when I launched my UFO Night Sky Watch Tour business in Hawaii (Big Island UFO Tours). It was one of those moments where a seemingly small decision alters the entire trajectory of your life.

Despite the struggles and challenging family dynamics, we kept choosing each other. The Sedona trip didn't destroy us. It changed the energy between us and stirred something I hadn't touched in a long time.

Six months after our private rooftop wedding in Thailand, we had a legal ceremony in Olympia, Washington, on June 22, 2019, at Burfoot Beach. Initially, Skip had not wanted to make the marriage official, but after the spiritual ceremony in Thailand, something shifted for him.

It was another midday wedding, simple and heartfelt. Our friend Chris officiated, and our only witnesses were my best friend Jen, Kylie (Chris and Jen's daughter), and my two children. That day was quiet, grounded, and sacred in its own way. Two souls affirmed what they already knew to be true.

Looking back now, I see how these adventures to Cancun, Belize, Sedona, Thailand, and beyond weren't just vacations. They were initiations. They marked thresholds in our journey. Each one brought joy, discomfort, clarity, or confrontation. Each one expanded who we were as individuals and as partners.

At the time, I thought we were seeing the world. Now I know we were also building our world.

CHAPTER 3

WHEN THE WORLD WENT STILL

A fter all the travel and the weddings, our life began to settle into something resembling a rhythm. Then the world changed. When the pandemic hit, everything compressed. Suddenly, we were all home, all the time. Skip's mortgage work went virtual. The kids were in online school full-time.

I was running both of my businesses, Design Smart and Mystic Manta, as best I could from home. Skip helped me with the vacant home staging jobs in the early days when there was still a lot of fear of being around people.

Every square foot of our house became multifunctional: classroom, office, gym, lunchroom, sanctuary, and battleground. The four of us, each with different needs and energies, tried to navigate uncertainty while sharing the same limited space.

Skip tried to be adaptable, but it wore on him. The constant background noise of Zoom calls and homework frustrations made it impossible to concentrate. He started escaping to his empty office building whenever he could, to breathe and feel some version of normal. That, in itself, said everything.

Tensions were high. It wasn't because we didn't love each other, but because there was no margin for peace. The walls felt smaller every day. The kids were wearing him down.

To make things harder, Skip struggled every winter in Olympia. The endless grey skies, cold rain, and lack of sunlight seemed to wrap around him like a heavy fog. What we thought was seasonal depression had been growing stronger each year. He'd become more withdrawn during the colder months. His usually vibrant energy was dimmed by the grey.

We often talked about creating a long-term plan, a 10-year vision to become snowbirds. We'd imagined escaping the winter months to find sun, somewhere warm and light. When the pandemic arrived, it provided the opportunity to rewrite that plan.

At the same time, life outside our home wasn't any easier. Early in the pandemic, my mother was diagnosed with breast cancer. She underwent surgery and needed time to recover, so she came to stay with us for a few days.

But like so many others at that time, the strain of too many people under one roof, combined with postoperative discomfort and stress, was too much. She ended up going back to her own house to heal on her terms. The emotional weight of her diagnosis hung in the background, quietly adding to the pressure we were all feeling.

And yet, even in the chaos, there were small bright spots. Mila turned into quite the baker. Every few days, she was whipping up some new dessert—cookies, brownies, and pies that filled the kitchen with warmth and sugar and the illusion of normalcy. It was one of the few things that brought us all together.

Then one night in May of 2020, we were sitting around the dinner table when Mila, in her usual boldness, said, "I don't want to live in Olympia anymore. I want to move to Malibu and be a surfer girl." I laughed because she wasn't even a strong swimmer, but her words landed.

My gut gave me the immediate answer, and I told her I'd never move to California (the water's too cold for me). Still, I paused and said, "I would move to Hawaii."

Skip looked at me and said, without hesitation, "I'd move to Hawaii too." That was the moment. What had once been a 10-year dream of chasing the sun became something more immediate. We made a two-year plan to get to Hawaii. It was just a seed of an idea, nothing too serious; however, the energy around it moved fast. The signs kept showing up in bumper stickers and other things related to Hawaii as I drove around Olympia. Six months later, in November 2020, we closed on a house on the Big Island. One month after that, we moved.

We had never seen the house we purchased in person, only via video tour. Because of Hawaii's mandatory two-week quarantine at the time, visiting beforehand wasn't realistic.

So instead, we binge-watched 13 seasons of *Hawaii Life*, trying to get a feel for the islands, studying neighborhoods, climate zones, and what kind of life might await us there.

Our very first trip together, early in our relationship, had been to Maui. We loved it, but Skip trusted me when I said the Big Island was where we needed to be. Maui and Kauai felt too small, and Oahu was too busy. I was the only one who had been to the Big Island before. I felt its energy. I knew it was where we would thrive.

During lockdown, we played games, exercised together, and tried to stay grounded. But deep down, we were restless. Our relationship had always thrived on expansion, movement, and discovery, and none of that existed inside those four walls.

Hawaii wasn't just a relocation; it was a lifeline. It was a return to the sun, to possibility, and a reset. We didn't know what would unfold on that island, but we knew we couldn't stay where we were. This was the in-between time. It wasn't quite an ending and not yet a beginning. It was our chance to step into something new.

CHAPTER 4

THE LEAP TO THE ISLANDS

Once the decision had been made, the move to Hawaii took on a life of its own. The energy accelerated, and so did the logistics. What no one tells you is just how many hoops you have to jump through to get animals into the state of Hawaii. It's not as simple as buying a plane ticket. There are health screenings, vaccinations, strict timelines, and a looming threat of mandatory quarantine if you miss even one detail. I was determined to get it all right. They were our family too, and I wasn't about to leave them behind.

On top of preparing the animals, there were the vehicles. Three cars and one motorcycle, each needing to be prepped and shipped across the Pacific. Then came the boxes. Forty of them. I mailed them all through USPS, packed with the most meaningful personal items: photos, sacred tools, keepsakes, and things too important to leave behind.

Everything else? I let it go. I sold or donated nearly everything else we owned, including furniture, dishes, décor, and clothing. It wasn't just about downsizing. It was about energetically starting fresh. I wanted our new home to hold only what mattered, with no clutter or old stories, just space for a new chapter.

Not everything went to plan, though. Initially, my son, Curran, age 12 at the time, was supposed to move with us. We had prepared for that, emotionally and logistically. We chose to purchase the bigger house so we could all be comfortable.

At the last moment, his father changed his mind and decided Curran couldn't go. It was heartbreaking. Our resources had gone into the move, and I didn't have the energy to fight with my ex over his decision. I had to surrender to something I couldn't control. I trusted that somehow it would still unfold the way it was meant to. Curran stayed with us in Hawaii for one week after we arrived before returning to Washington for school. That goodbye came too soon.

We arrived on the Big Island on December 28, 2020. As I stepped off the plane, I felt the energy shift immediately. The air was thick with humidity, plumeria, and salt. But more than that, it was alive. The mana of the island welcomed us in a way I can only describe as ancient, familiar, and benevolent.

We settled into our new home slowly. We slept on air mattresses for a couple of weeks until our new beds arrived. Our brand new furniture was delivered over time. Skip set up his office in a corner of the ohana, which also served as our bedroom. It wasn't ideal, but it worked. We made it work.

I started grounding again in ways I hadn't realized I was missing. My nervous system softened. With the lava beneath our feet, the openness of the land, the salt and sand, and the breathability of the sky, it all began to recalibrate me.

We watched the sunsets most evenings and lay under the stars, which was something we were not able to do in Washington during the winter. We were being retuned, rebalanced, and reborn. Hawaii was the place where something began to heal. Even our street name, Pau Nani, meant "a beautiful ending."

CHAPTER 5

WHEN THE SUN ISN'T ENOUGH

A t first, Hawaii was everything we dreamed it would be. We began each morning with birdsong and sunlight. The rhythm of the island was slower, softer, and for a little while, it felt like we had escaped the tension of our old life. The stress, the winter depression, and the confinement of four walls seemed to dissolve into ocean spray and lava rock.

There was joy in the simplicity. Early morning neighborhood walks, beach time, and stargazing were our simple pleasures. We marveled at the wild goats grazing by the road and watched geckos scurry across our walls. We opened the windows and let in the wind. We reminded ourselves that this was our life now. We did it. We made the leap.

But paradise doesn't protect you from pain. It just strips away the noise and makes the quiet parts louder. The island's energy, so intense and raw, amplified everything.

We were dealing with the challenging teen years. There was a particular instance I got a call from the school to pick up my daughter. Skip came with me as support, but that ended in an escalated fight between him and my daughter as I was driving her home.

Instead of softening toward her, he grew more reactive. He didn't know how to handle the volatility, the unpredictability, and the pain she was in.

He wanted to protect me, but his efforts backfired with sarcastic remarks, passive-aggressive comments, and childish retorts that only pushed her further away. A rift grew between them that never quite healed. It created a wedge between us as well.

Beneath it all, something in Skip was growing heavy. He had made friends on the island, but they weren't his people. They were not the deep, ride-or-die kind of friendships he had with his best friends, Tim and Jeff, back in Washington, who also both happened to be Canadian. He missed them fiercely. He missed laughing the way only they could make him laugh. He missed the ease, the loyalty, and the brotherhood. The connections he found on the island felt surface-level. They were friendly, but hollow. He wanted his new "Canadian" best friend.

Meanwhile, I was expanding in a completely different way. The island lit me up. I started meeting spiritually aligned women almost immediately. They were soul sisters, healers, and lightworkers. My intuitive gifts deepened. My connection to the unseen world strengthened. It felt like the island had welcomed me home on a soul level, and I was finally remembering why I came here.

That expansion created distance between me and Skip because we were evolving at different speeds and in different directions. Skip didn't quite know how to meet me in that spiritual space. I didn't know how to slow down enough to wait. I wasn't meant to slow down.

Work wasn't helping either. His mortgage job, which had been stable for years, became a source of growing frustration. It wasn't taking off the way he hoped it would. Deals fell through. Leads dried up. He began questioning everything. What he really wanted was a fun job on a golf course, but he didn't feel that would be a wise financial decision for our family.

Eventually, he switched to conducting home inspections and sales for Terminix, a pest control company, but that job came with its own stressors. He was gone for long hours and driving all over the island.

The emotional toll began to show. He would come home angry, particularly at the outdated technology he had to work with, which made his job twice as hard. Some nights, he tried to hide it. Other nights, he didn't. The island sun could only do so much. The cracks in our foundation were growing.

And yet, there were moments of light, especially at the beginning of my new business endeavor. In the summer of 2021, we launched my UFO Tour company here on the Big Island underneath my Mystic Manta LLC umbrella. It was something that had been seeded as an idea three years before, during our family trip to Sedona.

Skip was entirely on board and helped bring it to life. He worked all day in his job and then, at night, helped me with the tours. At first, it felt like a shared mission with adventure, excitement, and purpose. We were a team again, but over time, our differences began to show even in that space.

I wanted to speak about the spiritual side of galactic contact, including energy, consciousness, and higher-dimensional beings. Skip wanted me to stick to science, government disclosure, and technical validation. He supported me, but it became clear that he was uncomfortable with the metaphysical pieces of my message.

It led to small arguments, but nothing explosive, just little fractures in the connection. Skip would roll his eyes or push back when I talked about star families. I'd feel unseen and unheard. He didn't want me to lose credibility by going "too far out," and I didn't want to censor who I truly was. We started navigating two versions of reality, both valid and rooted in love, but sometimes fundamentally different.

Underneath that tension, money was becoming a silent storm. Back in Olympia, we had lived comfortably below our means. We had savings. We felt secure. Hawaii was different. The cost of living was higher, and our financial buffer started thinning.

Skip began expressing increasing concern. It wasn't just about bills. It was about stability and identity. He had always prided himself on being a provider and someone I could count on to contribute to the household. But here, he felt like we were falling behind.

His frustration began seeping into other parts of life. He supported me with my work, but I could tell he was disappointed that my business wasn't growing as fast as he had hoped. He was working long hours and still helping with my UFO tours at night. In the beginning, it had felt like something special we were building together. But over time, it became another point of friction.

As he grew more anxious, I felt more attuned. I could see the abundance everywhere. It appeared in the richness of the land, the soul-aligned people who were showing up in my life, and the steady unfolding of my purpose.

I felt held by something larger than circumstance, but Skip didn't see it that way. He saw rising grocery bills, a shrinking savings account, and a business that wasn't booming yet. The pressure mounted, and he carried it mostly in silence until it spilled out in irritability, anger, or long hours of withdrawal.

Through all of this, I kept expanding. The island wasn't just a new home. It was a mirror, a frequency, a portal, and a calling. It was awakening something in me that I couldn't ignore, and in doing so, it exposed everything that was no longer in alignment.

Even the love that had once felt like home began to feel unstable. I kept trying to hold it all together. The family. The household. My own unfolding spiritual mission. I didn't see what was coming, not fully. I just knew something was shifting underneath our feet, and I was holding my breath, hoping we'd find solid ground again.

CHAPTER 6

THE LAST PATH WE WALKED TOGETHER

Peru had intrigued me for years. It wasn't just about travel or adventure; it was a soul call. Something in me knew there was medicine waiting for me there. When the opportunity arose to travel with a group led by my friend and mentor Sunny, I said yes.

Skip came too, as I had just received a small inheritance from my grandfather's estate that was enough to cover the cost for both of us. He was willing to walk the sacred ground with me, though I'm not sure he understood just how transformative it would be.

But before we ever set foot in the Andes, there was turbulence at home. In April, just a few months before Peru, Skip's twin brother, Scott, and his girlfriend visited us in Hawaii for Skip and Scott's 54th birthday. We welcomed them into our home with love and hospitality, but from the beginning, the energy was off. This was the first time I had met either of them in person, so I wasn't sure what to expect.

Scott's girlfriend, who came from a small town in Ohio, seemed to arrive with certain expectations. She had heard our home's value and imagined we were living in a tropical mansion with a pool. When she saw our modest, cozy house without the luxury bells and whistles, her disappointment was obvious.

She offered no gratitude, just a quiet, passive disdain that colored the entire visit with whispered arguments behind closed doors with Scott. It got to a point where there was discussion of them getting a hotel room nearby, although that didn't end up happening.

Skip tried to keep the peace. In doing so, he ignored boundaries I had clearly set. During the second half of their visit, I was leading a spiritual healing retreat in Kona, so I was not staying at the house. Skip wanted to let them use our ohana, which was our sacred bedroom space. I was adamant that I would not allow them in our space. It was too personal.

Fortunately, he listened to me and had them continue sleeping in our spare bedroom. I also reminded Skip not to let them use my car, as it was having transmission issues and wasn't safe. I had rented a minivan to safely transport the women attending the retreat.

So when I was driving my retreat group from the airport and saw my car in front of us being driven by Scott and his girlfriend, my heart sank. I was livid. It wasn't just about the vehicle. It was about trust and about how often I felt my voice and intuition were brushed aside.

That week was hard. I was holding deep space for others in the retreat while carrying resentment and disbelief in my own heart. It was another fracture, minor, but meaningful.

During the retreat, I received a call from my aunt saying that my mother was in the hospital again, this time with a stroke, and that she might not live much longer. Immediately after the retreat, I flew back to Washington to get her affairs in order.

My mother didn't have a will in place or any advanced health directive, so I hired an attorney who drew up paperwork and came to the hospital for signatures. I decided to clean out her hoarder house and put it on the market, as I knew she would not be moving back in, even if she survived.

With the help of Jen and Chris, I was able to take care of everything in just two weeks. My mother stayed in the hospital for a couple of months. She recovered enough to eventually move into an independent living community apartment.

Then came Peru. We traveled with a group of 29 souls. I called it my Ancient Aliens tour of Peru, half joking but fully serious. I knew this journey wasn't just about ruins and megalithic structures. It was about memory and multidimensional truths hidden in stone.

Our first megalithic site was Ollantaytambo. As our guide, Alvaro, began the explanation of how the massive stones were supposedly moved, rolled across vast distances and up steep inclines using wooden logs, I couldn't hold back.

Under my breath, I was calling bullshit. Then I blurted out, "What about the Ancient Aliens?"

Skip was instantly irritated with me and embarrassed. He didn't like how bold I was about my beliefs, especially around strangers. I couldn't help it. The narrative didn't make sense, and I wasn't about to pretend otherwise.

Alvaro pulled me aside and smiled knowingly. "I'm with you," he said. "I just can't say it out loud on the formal tour." That one sentence changed everything. In Peru, tour guides are restricted by the government in what information they share, keeping it to a storyline that the Incas built these ancient sites only 600 years before.

For the rest of the trip, we opened up freely. Alvaro and I would exchange knowing looks and side conversations about galactic contact, higher intelligence, and the star races that once walked this Earth. We even talked about it as a group. It was like the veil dropped, and the real tour began.

Later on the trip, Alvaro introduced me to one of his artist friends who had an art gallery and studio we visited as a group. This man painted and sculpted otherworldly images, ETs, spacecraft, and cosmic landscapes.

When Alvaro told him about my connection to the Galactics, the artist's face lit up with recognition. He went into his office and came back with a gift for me, a Cintamani stone. He said it was retrieved from an ancient tomb and that the stone was of extraterrestrial origin. He placed it in my hand like a gift from the stars, a symbol of remembrance.

Meanwhile, Skip stayed on the periphery. He was kind and curious in his own way, and never outright dismissive. Still, I could feel him pulling back as if my expansion was creating distance he didn't know how to bridge.

Each person on our tour was allowed to ask Sunny one question to gain her psychic insight on. Everyone participated, except Skip. He stayed silent. I wasn't surprised, but I did feel the weight of it.

When it was my turn to ask Sunny a question, I asked about my business, specifically the abundance piece. Sunny had been my business mentor for several years, so I had an idea of what her response would be. I hoped her answer might ease some of Skip's stress about money.

She affirmed what I already knew: that I was exactly where I needed to be. The abundance would continue to unfold as I stayed aligned. She estimated that I would be at the same or even higher level of financial status as hers within five years or sooner. I don't think he really heard it, at least not in the way I wanted him to.

While I was receiving activations and forming soul bonds with members of the group, he remained slightly outside of it all. He was present but not fully plugged in. Looking back, I can see the threads unraveling. I was changing quickly and powerfully.

On our final day before getting on the airplane to return home, we visited the Tridimensional Stargate on the shore of Lake Titicaca. As I stood inside the stargate opening, I received a clear message from my Galactic team that I was on the right path and to stay focused on what I was doing. My timing was different from that of others. Peru wasn't just a journey. It was an activation.

It was the last trip of our shared human path before everything shifted. We had climbed the sacred stairs together, held hands under ancient skies, and received blessings, messages, and signs. When it was time to go home, I didn't quite know yet that we wouldn't walk the next chapter together.

CHAPTER 7

A RIFT BETWEEN REALITIES

Coming home from Peru felt like stepping through a portal. I wasn't the same woman who had boarded the plane. The sacred sites, the transmissions, and the stone-carried codes of Peru stirred something I hadn't fully accessed before. It wasn't just an upgrade. It was a deep remembering.

As soon as we landed back in Hawaii, the universe moved quickly to reflect that. A television show had contacted me prior to the Peru trip. They were doing an episode about UFOs in Hawaii. They wanted to feature my expanded spiritual UFO Tour.

The filming took place shortly after we returned from Peru. The timing felt divinely orchestrated. After all the initiations I had received in the Andes, I was stepping right into visibility, sharing my work with a broader audience, and anchoring my truth in front of the world.

Skip didn't want to be on camera. He supported me from the sidelines and told me how proud he was, but his energy was distant. He had already been retreating from the spiritual parts of the tour for a while, preferring that I focus on the science, the craft sightings, and government disclosure.

He struggled with how openly I spoke about multidimensional beings and galactic guides. He loved me for walking that path, but he couldn't fully walk it with me.

Around the same time, I met Chrystine. She was house-sitting for friends who had two dogs, one of whom was very ill. I felt called to help. I visited often, offering energy to the dog, who was holding on tightly, waiting for her people to come home before she could let go. I stayed with her, spoke to her, and held space in the way I knew how.

That's where I met JN. He was also helping Chrystine care for the animals. The three of us quickly formed a bond. JN and I clicked instantly, not romantically, but energetically. He was galactic too. When I talked about my experiences, he looked stunned, as if he was being seen for the first time. He told me he'd never met anyone like me before. He was excited to have someone like me with whom he could freely talk to about his experiences and share his photos.

It wasn't flirtation with JN. It was soul recognition. We were both married. There was nothing inappropriate. It just felt like finding a missing piece of my cosmic family.

Skip didn't see it that way. He picked up on the energy shift and asked questions that stemmed from fear. I reassured him, telling him nothing was happening between JN and me. But his jealousy had already taken root.

One morning, after listening to a voicemail that JN had left me the night before, Skip asked me to never speak to JN again. Even though the message was benign, I agreed.

It wasn't that JN didn't matter. It was because Skip did. I wanted to preserve our marriage, honor his request, and ease his worry, even if I knew the connection had been pure. I stepped back from that friendship and carried the ache silently.

That same day of the fated voicemail, I was preparing for my Galactic Retreat, which I was hosting in Hawaii in our neighborhood. A group of women had arrived on the island to journey into healing, activation, and multidimensional remembrance, and I was picking them up from the airport. I was ready to hold space.

But inside, I was stretched. I was mourning the rupture with Skip. I was recalibrating from the initiations in Peru. I was navigating the growing chasm between my public self, who was leading and thriving, and my private self, who was breaking. I did what I've always done. I compartmentalized. I led with love. I held space for everyone else while my own heart wobbled behind the scenes.

Skip and I were no longer on the same frequency. I was ascending into the unknown. He was sinking into fear. We were trying. We were loving. We were showing up. But we were no longer meeting in the same place. And I was beginning to wonder … How much longer could we keep walking together if we were facing opposite directions?

CHAPTER 8

THE MESSAGE I DIDN'T GET IN TIME

The Galactic Retreat began on Wednesday, September 13, 2023. I had picked up the group of women from the airport, ready to usher them into a multidimensional container of cosmic connection and soul remembrance.

These retreats were always transformative, not just for the participants but often for me as well. I was holding space for galactic awakening, while inside my personal world, things were unraveling in a way I couldn't yet comprehend.

The next day, the retreat officially began. That night, after our first full day of teaching and activation, Skip came over to the condo where we were staying. He said he wanted to talk about the situation with JN, as he had still been spiraling in fear and jealousy. We stood outside in the parking lot, finally able to take a breath and have a real conversation. His energy was softer than it had been in days. He said he was ready to move past the tension, specifically his jealousy about JN.

"I'll let it go," he told me. "I don't want to fight anymore. I want to be close to you again." We hugged, tightly, in a quiet moment of reconnection. It felt like healing was trying to happen. When Skip left that night, I believed we were on our way back to each other.

The next day, Friday, September 15, was busy. I was deep in retreat space, facilitating group energy work and holding the cosmic container with care. It wasn't until later that evening, after our night sky watch, that I finally picked up my phone.

That's when I saw it. Skip had sent me a text message earlier in the evening. It included a photo of the two of us, happy and laughing, from a moment that felt so full of love. Along with the photo, he had written that he wanted to come by that night to cuddle after our sky watch. He missed me.

My heart dropped. The message had come through more than two hours before I saw it. Immediately, I texted him back. I called. Nothing. No answer. I called again. Still nothing. I left a message and texted him to let him know he could come over. Tina, who was my assistant for the retreat, and her husband, Frank, were at the condo with me, sitting on the lanai, unwinding after the evening's session. It felt like Skip and I were on the edge of repairing something. I hoped he would come.

Tina then mentioned the eggs. She was telling Frank about our day and how we had made breakfast for the ladies. That triggered my memory that I had forgotten a second carton of eggs at home in the refrigerator. It gave me a reason to head home for a bit, to check in with Skip and have him come over to the condo, grab the eggs, and reset.

As I was driving home, Jupiter was shining brightly in the sky in the direction of our home. Something felt off. Around 9:30 p.m., I pulled into the driveway. I could see the blue tint of Skip's computer screen through the ohana window, just as it always looked when he was home working late.

I walked into the garage, where the eggs were waiting for me in the secondary refrigerator. After putting the eggs in the car, I walked out into the dark courtyard and immediately into the ohana where I expected Skip to be. What I didn't notice at the time was how dark the rest of the house was. Typically, there were different lights turned on throughout the home when we were there.

Jaxx, our Pomeranian, happily greeted me, tail wagging. Everything looked normal until it didn't. The space was empty. Skip wasn't at his computer. A barstool from our ohana kitchen island was in the middle of the floor. A ceiling fan had been taken down, but not replaced. I tried to turn the lights on, but they wouldn't turn on. A feeling crept into my stomach, tight, cold, and wrong.

I went into the family room, stepped out into the courtyard, and looked around. That's when I saw him. At first, it didn't register. He was sitting in a chair near the back corner by the ping pong table in the shadows, slumped. I thought maybe he had passed out from drinking too much, but as I got closer, I saw the blood. I thought maybe he was playing a sick joke on me. I reached out to him. He was cold. I screamed. I started pacing around the courtyard, as I was crying, in complete utter shock.

I dialed 911, my voice shaking, and my mind trying to process what my heart already knew. The dispatcher asked me who I needed: police, ambulance, or fire. I couldn't answer. I just told her my husband had killed himself. She stayed on the line with me. She suggested that I try to do CPR on him. I explained that it would not help, and I couldn't touch him in that way. He had shot himself in the head.

She asked if there was a weapon. I turned on my flashlight on my phone, and I saw the gun under the chair in the pool of blood. She told me to wait in the driveway and that help was on the way.

After the 911 call, I immediately called Tina. She and Frank arrived first. Mila came next, my beautiful daughter who had been through so much. She held me as I collapsed into her arms.

I couldn't understand it. Skip had made plans. He had wanted to come over that night. He wanted to be with me. Had I seen his message in time, would it have changed anything?

In the aftermath, it was as if I were playing Sherlock Holmes, trying to determine what had led to his decision. When I returned home a couple of days later, I learned about a bottle of pills he had secretly ordered. They were sex performance enhancers. He had never shared with me that he was concerned in that area. We had always had an active sex life. It reminded me of his concerns that he was aging too fast.

I thought I had loved him so thoroughly, so completely, but he couldn't fully receive it. Early in our relationship, he had flown to Arizona to get hair implants, as he was concerned about his hair loss and aging. He had me keep it a secret from our friends and family. He was always chasing something to make him feel better about himself, some version of himself he thought I deserved. He would often comment that I was getting younger and he was looking like an older man. I never asked for that. I loved him. All of him. He was my home. And now, he was gone.

I continued to lead the retreat, somehow, although the retreat turned into a different initiation. I stayed in that container of light for the women who had flown from the mainland, but something shifted deep inside me. I wasn't just holding space for others anymore. I was finally holding it for myself, inside a grief so immense it didn't have words.

In that rupture, something new began to form. This was not the way I would have chosen, but it was asking me to step into a new life, a bigger purpose, even if it meant walking forward without him.

CHAPTER 9

MESSAGES FROM THE OTHER SIDE

The night Skip passed, I returned to the condo where I was staying during the Galactic Retreat. My daughter, Mila, called my best friend, Jen, who lived in Olympia. Jen was still asleep when the call came through. She got the message the next morning and immediately booked a flight to Hawaii, arriving later that same evening.

That night, I lay in bed, spread out in a starfish configuration, barely able to process what had just happened. My physical body was in shock, but my energetic body was wide open. I could feel my Galactic team working on me, tending to the immense grief and trauma I had just experienced. Swirls of blue healing energy enveloped me as I surrendered into the strange, surreal quiet of that space. I wasn't alone. They were with me. I could feel them.

The morning after Skip's passing, the retreat ladies gave me space. I sat on the condo lanai looking at the trees and asked the question that echoed through my body. *Did it really have to be this dramatic? Did he really have to die?*

The answer came in a whisper, rustling through the trees: "Yes. It had to be this extreme to catapult you fully into your mission." That moment didn't erase the pain, but it gave it context. I could begin to make meaning. Deep inside, I knew I had just crossed into a new timeline, one I couldn't return from.

Jen's arrival grounded everything. She became my rock. She didn't ask questions. She showed up, making sure I ate, rested, and was held in love. She and one of the retreat participants, Wendy, performed an energy clearing ceremony at my house, guided by Sunny, who talked them through it over the phone. This was the day after Frank had graciously cleaned the courtyard, which took him several hours with bleach and pressure washing. I was beyond grateful I had rented the condos for us during the retreat, as I didn't have to return to the house right away. After the physical cleaning and energetic clearing, Mila and I could go back without feeling haunted by the residual imprint of what had occurred.

In the days that followed, messages started pouring in from the other side.

Psychic/Tarot/Oracle Card Reading with Cathy

The night after the energetic house clearing, one of my metaphysical friends, Cathy, did a tarot/oracle psychic reading for me. I didn't want her to focus on what had just happened. I wanted to know how I was going to move forward.

"He's not earthbound," she said. "He passed quickly. He's in the light. And he's already trying to help you." She started pulling cards, a blend of tarot and oracle decks. With each one, a new thread emerged.

The Lovers. "This is a soulmate card. Skip is saying you were the love of his life. He didn't always know how to show it, but it was real."

Throat Chakra. She paused. "His throat was blocked, not physically, but energetically. He had so much emotion that he didn't know how to express it. That's why he often kept things inside. It wasn't about you. He didn't know how to let it out."

Ten of Wands. "He carried so much burden. Generational pain. Emotional weight. It wasn't just recent. It's been a long time, and he didn't want to put it on you."

The Star. "He sees your path now. He understands your mission in a way he didn't before. He says he's going to help you now from the other side. He's one of your guides."

She saw him helping with my work. My galactic mission. The connections I was building. "He gets it now," she said. "And he's proud."

Justice. "This is about balance. Truth. Divine timing. Skip wants you to trust the unfolding of things. Even if it doesn't make sense right now.

"There will be someone else one day. Another partner. But Skip says only someone truly worthy. Someone who sees you fully. And he'll help guide that too."

The World. "You're completing a cycle. Travel will be part of your healing. It'll help you release the weight you've been carrying."

Knight of Cups. "Someone may approach you. Maybe symbolic of an apology. Or someone spiritual but slightly less mature. It could be a friend. Or something more. But you'll need to navigate it carefully."

She reminded me I was coming through as the **Queen of Pentacles**, stable, grounded, protected.

Sacral Chakra, Solar Plexus, Third Eye. "Your creativity and life force are coming back online," she said. "Your galactic energy is waking up again. You're being called to take a risk, to follow where the fireworks are."

The Vast Universe. "It's both galactic and international. You're being pulled into your bigger purpose.

"There's a new connection coming. Possibly a business partner, possibly a friend, possibly more. Someone who doesn't take energy from you, but amplifies it. Someone who supports your light."

Immortal, Snowflake, Guilt, The Moon. "There's complexity around you. Pressure from others. You're in a fragile state right now, but it's giving you clarity. Someone may show up with an apology, possibly Skip, possibly someone else. There's guilt, emotional confession, a desire to reconnect."

She saw spring as a key season. The energy would begin shifting then. "This next phase will ask you to be bold. There's a timeline jump happening. A gamble, a leap of faith. And it brings in something new."

Dreams Coming True. "Your heart's desires are manifesting. But some bridges will never be crossed again. You're not going back."

Then came the conversation about deception. Cathy saw people approaching during this time of vulnerability, some with good intentions, others with ill intentions.

"There's someone coming through around the time you receive a gift or inheritance. Possibly a masculine figure. Possibly connected to business. There could be jealousy or attempts to interfere. Shield your energy."

She emphasized confidentiality. "There may be private meetings. Agreements. Someone wealthy is helping fund a new venture. But others are watching. Jealous. Suspicious. Some may try to push you away, energetically or literally."

The Star (Again), The Wheel of Fortune, The Sun. "Your destiny is unfolding. There's abundance coming. Success. But also a reminder: Be wise about who you share it with."

Cathy looked at me and smiled. "He's got your back. And you've got work to do. He's going to help with all of it."

Psychic/Mediumship Reading with Lisa Holm

A week later, in a session with my friend and teacher Lisa Holm, a gifted psychic medium, Skip came through clearly.

"He's already here," she said. "He showed up before we even got on the call."

"He's in so much joy," she said, smiling. "He's literally bouncing in. He can't wait."

Right away, he said, "I love you. You were the love of my life. I know you're mad. I know it was a shitty thing to do. But I couldn't keep going."

Lisa paused, letting it land. "He said he just didn't have it in him anymore. That you were the one who always made things work."

"You're strong," he said. "You have the fire. You have the drive. I didn't."

Then, almost bashfully: "They became my kids too."

"He says he tried to do it as simply as possible," Lisa added. "He didn't want to traumatize anyone. He didn't want you or the kids to find him."

She was quiet for a moment. "Did he take pills?"

"No. He shot himself."

"Oh," she said. "That makes more sense. I saw something with the head, but he didn't want to show it to me clearly. He's very gentle. I think he was trying to protect me."

"He's saying: You need to know you didn't cause this. There was nothing you could've done to stop it."

Lisa's voice softened even more. "He had been thinking about it for a long time. Years, actually."

"He's around you a lot. Especially when you're doing your work."

"He's saying: You were never supposed to stop. And now you won't."

"He's helping with your work. He says he couldn't handle the mission in his human form, but he can from the other side."

Lisa relayed that he had met guides. That he was learning. He understood things now that he couldn't see before.

"And he's amazed by you," she said. "He's saying, 'She's going to do even more now. And I get to help.'"

Lisa looked at me and said, "He's proud. And he's saying something about the galactic work. He gets it now. He knows it's real. He's going to help bring people to you. People who need it. People who are ready."

Before we ended the session, Lisa offered one last message: "He says you will love again, but only someone truly worthy of you. Don't settle. Don't choose someone just because they seem spiritual. Choose someone who shows up. Who walks beside you fully."

"He'll help with that too."

Readings and Messages From Others

In the days that followed, other friends and intuitive colleagues shared nearly identical messages without knowing what had already come through. They all saw new love and partnership on the horizon, part personal, part spiritual, and potentially part business. They also echoed Skip's sentiment: that he had been unintentionally holding me back with his fears, and that his absence was removing that block.

Everything had changed. And still, something deeper within me whispered, *You're going to be okay.* Skip may have left the Earth plane, but his spirit was working overtime on the other side, loving me, encouraging me, making good on his promise: "I'll be around, Lisa. You'll feel me. But now, it's time for you to rise."

CHAPTER 10

SIGNS FROM THE OTHER SIDE

In the quiet aftermath of Skip's passing, I was raw, aching, and unsure how to move through each day. Yet even in the thickest fog of grief, I began to notice signs and whispers from the unseen that Skip wasn't entirely gone.

It started with the cockroaches. Roughly two weeks after his passing, I began to notice them. Giant cockroaches, a couple of inches long, showed up in my ohana bathroom.

There wasn't just one or two, but nine of them, all within 24 hours. This was highly unusual. In Hawaii, it's not uncommon for a stray cockroach to fly into the house occasionally. But this was different. These weren't random. They had a presence and a message.

I showed them to Jen, who had become my steady anchor through this new reality. "Look at this," I told her. "This can't be a coincidence."

My intuition nudged me to look deeper, so I did what I often do in moments like this. I turned to the spiritual meaning. I Google-searched for "spiritual significance of cockroaches," and the answer that popped up hit me like lightning: *Indestructible. Survivor. Able to endure anything.*

It was Skip. I knew it in my heart. He was reminding me I could survive this, and that I would survive. I was indestructible, even if I didn't feel that way at the moment. It was such a Skip way to deliver a message. After all, he had worked for Terminix. Pest control was his latest profession.

Now, his presence was showing up through some of the very creatures he had spent his workdays trying to help people eliminate from their homes. Once I acknowledged the message, the cockroaches stopped coming. Just like that, no more cockroaches appeared in my room, not a single one.

The signs didn't stop there. Another came in the form of a smell, one I knew all too well. One evening, I was sitting alone in the ohana, wrapped in memory and aching for his presence, and then I smelled it. Dirty socks. That unmistakable, pungent smell that used to waft through the house when Skip got home from work, kicked off his shoes, and let his feet breathe. I laughed through my tears. "Really, Skip?" I said out loud. "That's the smell you're sending me?"

Still, I knew it was him. It was another confirmation. He was reaching through the veil with what he had. But I did ask him to pick a different scent next time, one a little more pleasant. Not long after, he did.

The smell shifted to that of marijuana. The next scent that wafted through had surrounded him in life. Skip had been a daily pot smoker, and even though I didn't partake, the smell had become part of the texture of our life together. Now, it was floating into the room without a source. It came as a sweet, smoky reminder that he was close.

One day, not long after that, Jen and I went to the beach to ground and heal. The sand was warm beneath my feet, and the ocean stretched out endlessly before us. I sat still in my chair, letting the elements do their healing work. Jen excused herself for a few minutes, and as I was sitting there alone, I saw him.

He was not in his usual human form, but as a massive energy being, tall, luminescent, and powerful. His presence radiated love and support. He was reminding me of the bigger picture, of our soul connection, and of the roles we had played for each other, even beyond this lifetime.

I could feel him everywhere—on the beach, in the car, and even in the chimes that rang in the breeze when no one else was around. He sent me songs through the Depeche Mode Pandora station. Each lyric felt like a message.

I danced. I cried. I voice-memoed my thoughts at night when the silence was too loud. And always, I listened in the stillness for him. Skip was gone, and yet he wasn't. He was dancing in and out of dimensions, sending me signs through the natural and the supernatural alike, through bugs, smells, and energy. I was learning to listen.

Skip Helping Others from Across the Veil

Skip and I had a mutual real estate agent friend, Leiola, who shared with me that she had a few interactions with Skip after his passing. She wrote up the scenarios for me, which I share below:

Blessed by Skip #1

My first interaction with Skip was the Tuesday after he passed. It was mid-morning, and I suddenly felt the urge to stop what I was doing, so I did.

At that moment, I felt that Skip was there. I focused and received that he was trying to communicate to me that he was okay. That he was calm and that I could be okay because he was calm and he was okay. I felt peace and contentment in that moment. The moment passed. I acknowledged my appreciation and moved on with my day.

That night, I saw Skip's face in my dream. It was just his face, and as I looked at it, I could see the same calm and okay look and feeling that he had been relaying to me earlier that day. Just confirmation that it was indeed him earlier that day, and that I could be calm and okay, and I should share this with you when I saw you, which I did when I saw you at Skip's celebration.

Blessed by Skip #2

The following night, I was emotionally drained, stressed, and upset as I was racking my brain all day on a real estate issue that involved my family. As the one everyone comes to for all their real estate problems, despite having all the resources, I just could not figure out how to solve this one.

Then, while I was relaxing before I went to bed, Skip just popped into my head and gave me the key to solving that problem. It was, as they say, like a light bulb went off, but in the same instant that the light bulb went on, I received that it was Skip who turned it on for me.

I jumped up from where I was sitting and immediately told Jamie that I had the answer! You should have seen how shocked he was that I went from exhaustion and on the verge of falling asleep to being awake, elated, and excited all of a sudden. Skip had done that for me!

Blessed by Skip #3

To set the scene for this next part, I had been struggling with one of my properties that had been listed for sale, but still hadn't sold. I had given the listing to another company (rather than listing it myself, which I should have done from the start), who said if I wanted it sold within three months, I should let them list it, and it would sell at $1.5M.

Well, it was now six months later. I had dropped the price and told the agent to bring me an offer, ANY offer, but still, no offer despite their continued confidence that they could sell it for me.

At Skip's celebration, I had told you about Skip helping me with my previous real estate issue, and you had said that Skip had been helping you and Jennifer with lots of different things and that I could ask Skip to help with even more! So I did.

The next day, Monday, I asked Skip to help with the property that hadn't sold. The property had been looming over our heads and was the source of extreme stress at this point.

I wanted the property gone, sold, and done with, so I asked Skip for some very specific things.

1) I asked for a sales price of $1M.

2) I asked for an offer in the next day or two.

3) I asked for a quick close.

4) I asked for it to be a cash sale.

Please, please, please, Skip, help me out and work your magic!

It was now Tuesday. I got a call from a friend that her client might have her write an offer. The following day, the other company, who I had listed the property with, said they were also working on an offer. Wow, Skip! I asked for one and I'm getting TWO?!? Like the DAY after I asked you to help!

However, in my world, unless it's on paper, it isn't real. So I waited for a contract to come in.

A few hours later, sure enough, Skip came through for us. Now, how do I know it was Skip? Well ...

1) I had asked for the offers to come in in the next day or two, and that's exactly when they came in.

2) The offer price was $1M, just as requested.

3) The offer was a cash offer, just as requested.

4) The offer happened to come from someone who was my friend, but who ALSO knew Skip! It came from realtor Bherin Brown, who had also used Skip for termite inspections.

5) If there was any doubt that it was Skip working on this for me, this last piece confirmed it … our closing date … was set for Halloween!

As it turned out, we ended up closing escrow early, but I know this was Skip working beautiful magic for his friends.

I also had this feeling at the time that Skip had been very, very powerful up there, but that at some point, he would be called away from helping us here in the earth realm as there were other and more important things to work on.

I feel blessed and am so very appreciative that he chose and was able to help me with not one, but two BIG, life-changing blessings.

Blessings to you and your ohana, Lisa. Skip is so special, and I mahalo you for supporting and loving him.

And to Skip … "MAHALO PIHA!!!"

CHAPTER 11

HOLDING BOUNDARIES, HOLDING MYSELF

In the days following Skip's death, the emotional terrain was unlike anything I had experienced. There was the grief, the shock, and the quantum upheaval. Jen stayed with me for three weeks until an emergency situation in Olympia called her back home.

She made sure I was eating, sleeping, and functioning. We went to the beach nearly every day to let the ocean transmute our pain. I canceled all of my UFO tours. I unplugged from the world. I surrendered to the profound healing unfolding on every level, including physical, emotional, spiritual, and galactic. She acted as my gatekeeper, holding the field of love and helping me protect my peace.

What I hadn't fully prepared for was navigating the emotions of others, in addition to my own. Everyone meant well. But even well-meaning energy can be heavy when you're in a delicate state. Some came to me with tears and heartbreak in their eyes, radiating pain that wasn't mine to carry. Others were angry at themselves, at Skip, or at me.

One friend bluntly told me, "This is going to suck for a long time." I looked her in the eye and said, "No, it's not. That's not the reality I'm choosing." Because the truth was, I knew I was walking through a sacred fire. I wasn't going to let anyone else define how I moved through it.

Even during Skip's Celebration of Life on the beach, I had to stay grounded in my own frequency. Most people came with respect, but some comments and energies felt misaligned. One person wondered aloud how I would survive financially, assuming Skip had been the breadwinner. That wasn't our reality. And yet, their assumptions said more about them than me.

The most difficult interaction came from Skip's twin brother, Scott. In the hour or two before his death, Skip had tried to call him, but it went to voicemail. His brother didn't hear the message until the next morning. When I finally remembered Skip's phone passcode a few days later, I called him back. I shared the news as gently as I could.

After that initial conversation over the phone, he didn't want to communicate via talking, only texting. What came through was a wave of anger, blame, and unmet expectations. He was upset that I hadn't put together a formal funeral with the family involved. I told him that was not my job and not what Skip would have wanted or expected. I hosted a Celebration of Life on the beach, open to all, which was followed by a more intimate gathering in October around Halloween. I invited Scott to come to the Halloween celebration, but he chose not to. He was angry that I was acting as if I were moving on with my life.

I offered to send him some of Skip's ashes so he could hold his own ceremony if he wanted. He never gave me his address to do so. At some point, I had Jen text him on my behalf because I couldn't endure his angry rants. That made him even more furious. I made it clear that I would only continue the conversation by phone, not by text. That was my boundary. He never replied again.

Skip's brother may have needed someone to blame. That someone was me. And while I understood the grief and guilt that can twist into misplaced rage, I wasn't willing to be the target of it. I've learned this before: what other people think of me is none of my business. Their pain doesn't override my peace.

Another firm boundary had to be set with one of Skip's female friends from Olympia. She completely stepped out of line by demanding information about his death. I told her I didn't have to answer her questions. Fortunately, some of her other friends talked her out of attacking me. They asked if they could hold a celebration in his honor in Olympia, which I, of course, said yes to.

There's a societal script around grief. People expect it to look like complete collapse, endless mourning, and isolation, but I knew better. I had chosen a quantum path. I knew that Skip was free and that he was with me. His death wasn't the end. It was a change in form.

He told me in that first week, through Lisa, the medium, "You don't have to grieve for long. I don't want you to. You're meant to keep living your life." And I listened.

During the three weeks with Jen, she helped me begin the process of reclaiming our space. Our bedroom became mine again. As a former interior designer and energy worker, I knew that the faster I shifted the environment, the easier it would be to change the energy. We donated Skip's clothing and sorted through his belongings. Every item released created more space for light.

This chapter of grief wasn't about spiraling downward. It was about rising to the strength I had cultivated all along. The boundaries I set weren't to keep people out. They were there to keep me whole, so I could rise and heal. I could keep walking my mission because Skip wasn't gone. He was just transformed and cheering me on from a different dimension.

CHAPTER 12

THE KINDNESS THAT CARRIED ME

In the days following Skip's passing, I was stretched in ways I never imagined possible. And yet, amid the unimaginable, something profound emerged. There was a flood of love and support from the community I had cultivated over the years on the island.

For most of my life, I had trouble asking for help. I was raised to be fiercely independent. My mother taught me that relying on others was a sign of weakness. It took decades for me to unlearn that belief. When Skip transitioned, I didn't even need to ask. People showed up.

Jen was the first, as I've previously shared. I didn't need to ask her to come. She simply got on the airplane to be by my side. She became my anchor. She was more than a best friend. She became my gatekeeper, shielding me from unnecessary energy and allowing space for my healing.

Others stepped in too. Diandra, a fellow member of my local BNI group, organized a meal train. Meals began arriving at our doorstep along with envelopes of money from people who wanted to support us in any way they could.

My dear friend and mentor, Sunny, created a donation page through her non-profit, and the generosity from her community moved me to tears.

People who had never met me gave from the heart. Some donations and gifts came with beautiful messages of encouragement and love.

The ripple of support reached far and wide beyond Hawaii, beyond even my own networks. It reminded me that love doesn't always arrive through familiar faces. Sometimes it finds you through the kindness of strangers. Sunny also gathered a team of powerful energy healers to work with both me and Skip across dimensions. Her steady presence and energetic care were invaluable.

Meanwhile, my friend Jodie, from North Dakota, texted me every single day, checking in, holding space, and reminding me I wasn't alone. Most of my wider circle gave me space, holding me in quiet love from afar, just the way I needed.

There were also practical needs. Skip had left behind three vehicles: a Jeep, a motorcycle, and a partially disassembled 1972 BMW "project" car that had lived in the garage for years, both in Olympia and Hawaii.

Before I could sell them, I had to transfer the titles into my name, which meant finding the missing license plates for the BMW. Jen took on that mission for me and asked Skip for help. She was guided to exactly where the plates were in two different hiding places. She found them on the first try. That moment felt like magic. It was also pure Skip.

The BMW was the first vehicle to sell. Jen encouraged me to trade in my car with the transmission issues for a new one, now that I didn't have Skip as backup help if the car broke down. We met our friend Anthony at the BMW dealership, and I test-drove a couple of cars.

He introduced me to Sean, the finance manager, who had actually met Skip and knew about the 1972 project car. Sean scheduled a time to see the car and agreed to take it off my hands. I was more than happy to take his cash offer to get it out of the garage.

Anthony stepped in to help sell the Jeep, as neither Mila nor I wanted to keep it. He listed it on social media and showed it to potential buyers, so I didn't have to deal with potential buyers alone. After a couple of weeks, I met with a buyer from my network of contacts at Anthony's workplace and released it with love.

The motorcycle was the last to sell. Mila's boyfriend's dad helped show the motorcycle to a couple of his friends, but it wasn't the right fit. Several months later, it was sold, thanks to Isaiah, who mentioned it to a coworker. It took a team to move things forward.

Then there was another form of support, which I didn't expect, but one I deeply appreciated. Before I could find a regular yard person, my daughter's boyfriend's family stepped up. Tanu, his dad, and their family friend came over and helped clear the overgrown yard. They trimmed, hauled, and cleaned up the outdoor space that Skip used to tend to.

It was more than just yard work. It was an act of kindness and care that I will never forget. In those moments, I felt held not just by my own network but by the extended community that surrounded my children.

These moments became evidence of spiritual support and Skip's ongoing presence. He was still showing up in his loyal, goofy, and supportive way, just in a different form. This chapter of my life was one of heartbreak, yes, but also one of grace and allowing. I realized I was held by more than just angels and galactic teams. I was also held by humans who loved me, and that, too, was part of my healing.

CHAPTER 13

THE UNANSWERED WHY

Grief after suicide is a different kind of storm. It doesn't move in clean lines. It circles and revisits. It throws debris from every direction: shock, guilt, anger, deep sorrow, and, most persistently, a desperate need to understand why.

In the days and weeks following Skip's death, that question looped through my mind endlessly. He hadn't left a note, a message, or anything to help piece together the final moments of his decision. What remained was a swirl of fragmented conversations, subtle shifts in his energy, and the hindsight of signs that I didn't fully recognize at the time.

There were things we knew. He struggled with anxiety. He felt the pressure of finances. He was deeply dissatisfied with his work life. There was also the way the island magnified both our spiritual paths and our emotional challenges. He hadn't fully landed in the joy of his new life in Hawaii. But were they enough to push someone to the edge?

The truth is, I don't know. Some days, I believe that his soul made a conscious exit. It was an agreement from a higher level that this was the only way I would fully step into my mission. On other days, I feel the raw human pain of abandonment and the ache of a life interrupted too soon. There is a haunting sensation that maybe, just maybe, something more could've been done. This inner pendulum swing between spiritual understanding and human devastation is the rhythm of grief after suicide.

I've spoken with others who have walked this road. Each story is unique, but there's a common thread. There is the longing to go back, to do something differently, and to fix what cannot be fixed. The heart replays conversations and rewrites history in search of answers it may never receive.

I've received messages from Skip through mediumship and signs in the physical world, which act as reminders that he is still around in a different form, and he sees things clearly now. He loves me. He's sorry. And yet, even with those beautiful validations, the grief remains. They don't cancel each other out. They coexist. One doesn't erase the other.

Over time, I've come to understand that asking "why" isn't about solving a mystery. It's about bearing witness to the weight of love and loss. It's about staying present to the complexity of being human.

Skip's death shattered something in me, but it also opened something new, a threshold I didn't know I was standing at. As much as I wish the doorway could've opened another way, I'm slowly learning to walk through it with my heart wide open and compassion for myself, for Skip, and for anyone who's ever been left wondering why.

CHAPTER 14

WHAT I SAID WHEN NO ONE WAS LISTENING

In the days and weeks after Skip passed, I found myself talking into my phone, trying to catch what was moving through me before it disappeared. Some days I was angry. Some days I was numb. Other times, I'd feel him so close I could hardly breathe. These voice memos weren't meant for anyone else. They were just me, mid-process, trying to make sense of the impossible, stay connected, and survive.

Listening back, I can see how my understanding shifted over time, and how grief moved in waves. The truth revealed itself slowly. The recordings were raw, unfiltered moments from those early days, pieces of my heart, spoken out loud.

I'm including some of them here and in the following chapters because they tell the truth of my experience and understanding beyond this physical life in a way nothing else does. This is the reality of what it felt like to be in it. My hope is that if you're walking through your own version of this kind of grief, hearing these moments might help you feel less alone. I also include them because even in my deep sadness, I had some profound insights that helped me move forward day by day.

October 3, 2023

Jen bought me the most amazing photo by Jean Luc. In the photo, you're this happy, smiling dolphin. And honestly, that's how I see you now: pure joy. Just playful, just light. Based on your last messages to me, that's how I picture you: free, joyful, back in your true essence.

Earth life? Fun, but hard. And I'm still here. You gave me permission to have fun, and I'm choosing to take you at your word. That doesn't mean I don't miss you in every single moment, every day. But I know life goes on here. People die all the time. It's part of what we do as Earth humans. One day I'll die too, and I'll be where you are. I wonder what that will be like, whether you'll reincarnate again here on Earth, or whether you'll stay as pure energy for a while.

Since Earth operates in such linear time, maybe you can help confirm this for me on your side. I still want to write books with you. I've agreed to that. And I know we'll need to wait until I'm ready to fully connect, but I'm genuinely excited about that idea.

Now, a question: Does this mean we put the whole UFO thing on pause? Because I can't switch gears again so suddenly. My whole life has been shift, shift, shift … nonstop. And I thought we were doing this thing, the real, grounded, no-fear, galactic-contact, extraterrestrial-awareness thing. Maybe we still are. Maybe we aren't. I'm just going to stay open to the flow. As long as it's flowing, and as long as it's rooted in beauty and purpose, I'll keep going.

I know we were more aligned than you realized. We had different comfort zones, but we got each other. I see that now.

Miss Bindy (my cat) is on my lap right now, licking me, rolling around. It feels like one of my little love letters to you, babe. Because honestly, it's always you. It's always been you.

That weekend before you left, I got to see it so clearly. I saw the little blips of reality shifting. None of this is solid. None of it is ultimately real. It's all just some wild tangent of experience. But we? We are eternal. We are souls. And I know not everyone gets that.

Some people get stuck in who they think they are in this 3D version of reality, and they forget that it's all temporary. But not us. We knew.

I don't think I recorded this last night, but I rearranged the entire ohana. I moved furniture and cleared things out again. I needed to. And one of our friends said to me, "This is going to really suck for a while." But I'm so grateful I'm spiritually advanced enough to know it doesn't have to.

I'm so glad I chose to get a reading from Lisa. You came through so clearly and reminded me that it's okay to be happy sooner than later. It's okay not to grieve forever. Everyone else probably knew that. But having your permission helped me actually believe it.

So when that friend said that to me, that it's going to suck, I got to pull out one of my own phrases, one I used during the galactic retreat. I asked her, "Do you want to reframe that?" Because my reality is not that this sucks.

My reality is: everything is moving, and everything is flowing smoothly. That's what I choose. And to her credit, she reframed it. I'm not sure she believes it yet, but it's okay. Everyone's on their own journey. Everyone has their own way of navigating a polarized 3D Earth.

And I know we're shifting to 5D now. Even this, even your death, is part of that shift.

Maybe we set this up beforehand. Maybe you offered to play this role for me in this life. To fall in love with me more deeply than either of us ever had in Earth form. Because in the spiritual realm, we already were that.

You said it, or Lisa did for you. "Thick as thieves." That's us. It's always been you and me, babe.

And then Earth School happened. You left halfway through. We only met eight years ago. We were late bloomers. We chose hard things. But we met. We fell in love. And it was beautiful. Even though it got confusing at the end … It was still pure love.

I keep telling Jen I've got 50 years left. Maybe more. I'm halfway through life. Three husbands, four careers, two kids. Most people don't fit that into one life, let alone one lifetime's halfway point.

I understand where you are now. And I understand, at least in part, why you did what you did. I also understand why people around me don't. But I want to thank you for coming through to explain it. Through Lisa. Through Sunny. Through others.

Because, babe, your friends are carrying so much guilt. And they shouldn't be. You were such a good friend to them. A real listener. A deep soul. For some of them, you were the most enlightened person they had ever known. Please know you made a real impact. Even with your own struggles, your heart was huge. And they miss you so deeply.

But I know you're not in the vase I picked out for your ashes. I know you're in the energy of this space. That's why I can talk to you like this. Still, I kept the vase because I like mementos. I'm visual. You know that.

I created a little display in the car so you can ride with me. We have a new BMW now. I sold Dixie (Skip's 1972 project BMW). Jen calls the new one "Baby Pele." She's taking good care of me. And you? You're my co-pilot.

I also got the crystal. The Andara. It helps me connect with you, and with the higher realms.

I'm keeping my energy clean. When people come at me with lines like "this is going to suck," I just don't take it in. That's their reality, not mine.

Your brother, unfortunately, is in that loop. And yes, we used to argue about his trip. That was a tough moment in our relationship. But we got through it.

Skip, I love you.

And yes, I'm ready. I want you to come through to me more. I want to write the books. The anger? I'm done with it. You thought I was mad, but really, I was just handling it. Getting shit done.

The ceiling fans? Two are fixed. Chris is doing the other four.

The BMW in the garage, the one torn apart? It's gone. Thank you, Sean. And thank you, Skip. I know you helped with that.

The hardest part is over. The other things? They're falling into place. You said we'd be fine financially. I believe you.

I've changed the room. I've changed the energy. I have an altar to you, at least for now. It feels good. And when the time is right, I'll take it down. But you will never be replaced in my heart.

You gave me permission to love again. It came through in a tarot reading right after you passed. I know it'll happen when the time is right.

And I want you to know … that love will just be another expression of you because you are my love. And everything that happens next comes from that love. You deserve love just as much as I do. Because you are me. And I am you.

As I speak this, I'm getting that same feeling in my body I had in that vision a week before you left. That dream where I saw so clearly who we were together, walking this multidimensional path.

It's true. You are me. I am you. I love you. I love you. I love you. You are the love of my life. You are the love of my dreams. You are the love of the universe and beyond. Thank you for showing up in my life. Thank you for reminding me of who I am. That's who I am now. And that's who I'm becoming.

CHAPTER 15

FEELING GRATEFUL

The next day, there were two different transmissions I shared via voice memo. To summarize:

Today was one of those days where gratitude filled every part of me. I felt so thankful for the love I've received, for the friends and mentors who've held me, and most of all, for the kind of love I got to experience with Skip. Not everyone gets that in this life.

I've also been thinking a lot about guilt and how so many of us wonder if we could've done more, loved better, or seen the signs. But I know, deep down, that we all played our roles exactly as we were meant to. Even me. Even Skip. His pain ran deep and long before I entered the picture.

While I miss him terribly, I also see the perfection in the way it all unfolded. His essence is still with me. The signs, the visits, the ongoing love, they're real. This chapter of my life is full of endings and beginnings, tears and transformation. And as much as I've been grieving, I'm also rising. I'm reconnecting with Earth, channeling deeper truths, feeling the dragons stir. I'm not here to grieve by the book. I'm here to feel, to witness, and to grow. I am also here to help others do the same.

October 4, 2023

Today I'm really feeling gratitude. Deep, anchored gratitude. I'm so grateful for the love and support I've received from my friends, my mentors, and my teachers. I'm especially grateful that I got to experience a kind of love in this life that not everyone gets to feel.

Coming to Earth is no small thing. But Skip loved me in ways I had never been loved before. He understood my love languages. He consciously went out of his way to make sure I felt loved. And I did the same, to the best of my ability.

But here's something I've realized. We can only receive love to the degree that we have it within ourselves. So even when we're giving love in the way the other person receives it, they may not fully take it in because they don't fully believe they're worthy of it. That's not something we can control.

I've had several conversations lately about guilt, about people wondering if they could've done something different. Better. "I should've reached out more." "I should've been a better friend." But the truth is, everyone played their role perfectly. Each person did exactly what they were meant to do within their soul contract.

We all agreed to this before we came here. Whatever the lesson, whatever the moment, even if we were background characters, we all signed up for our parts. Maybe it's all running simultaneously in a multidimensional way, which is what I believe. But regardless of how it plays out, no one is to blame.

Some people have wanted to place guilt on me too, especially since Skip and I were having a little bit of a hard time right before he passed. But it was a complete misunderstanding. I can't remember all the details, so I'm not going to beat myself up about that. I shared my truth, what I knew at the time. And later, I gained even more clarity.

The issue he was so upset about wasn't what he thought it was. What I saw was a spiritual epiphany, a deeper truth being revealed. It had nothing to do with what Skip may have perceived. That incident was just the final cherry on top of what had already been building for years.

When he came through to me, he said it clearly. This pain had been going on for a long time. It wasn't about me. It was about not feeling lovable. Not feeling worthy. He had this inner need to prove himself through being a provider, being the breadwinner, being the "good husband."

But then he met me, and I made more money. I'd done that most of my life. I was used to standing on my own. So the pressure he put on himself to "catch up" or "be enough" only grew. Through multiple readings, he's confirmed that he felt like he couldn't gain traction, like he was past his prime and unable to grow in the way he saw me growing.

It wasn't anyone's fault. So for those carrying guilt, especially his brother, who may think he should've returned that call, please know that nothing was said or unsaid that could have stopped it. Skip wasn't in the spiral yet. He simply texted, "Call me when you get a chance." It wasn't a cry for help.

I've talked to my daughter about this. I've talked to friends who've considered leaving this life, or even attempted to. What I've learned is that nothing anyone says or does can prevent someone from choosing to go if their soul has made that decision.

We are all playing our roles to perfection. We can think, "I should have … I could have …" but it happened exactly the way it was meant to happen. I know that's hard to accept. Especially when the death comes out of nowhere, when there were no big signs of depression, no suicidal threats. He never said a word about it. And yet, sometimes those are the exact people who leave. We don't really know what's going on inside someone, not even when we're married to them. Not even when we see them every day. And maybe we're not supposed to.

The real question is: now that it's happened, how do we respond? Do we live differently? Do we show up more? Do we stop waiting for the perfect time to do what we've been dreaming about? Because if I've learned anything in 50 years on this planet, and I plan to live another 50, maybe even 100, it's this: live your life. Whatever you're afraid of, do it anyway. You never know when your time will come.

Skip left behind a lot of unfinished things. And yeah, when he came through my friend Lisa, he said, "I know you're mad at me." And I was. I'm devastated. My husband, my best friend, is gone. But I was mad, too. Because he left laundry in the washer. He never does that. He used to get upset with my daughter for doing that. He left ceiling fans half-installed, car projects half-finished, loose ends everywhere.

He had called the plumber. He'd asked our friend Bill for help. He was making plans. Which is why it's so clear this was a perfect storm, not a long-planned exit, but an accumulation of pressure, self-doubt, and emotional pain that became too much.

It happened. And as much as we want to rewind and redo it, we can't. But he's not gone. Skip was never just the body. That was the costume. His essence remains. He is energy now. He's Source. He's multidimensional.

So when people tell me, "He visited me," I say, "Of course he did." He helped my best friend find license plates in the garage. He helped me find the push pins for the Halloween lights. These signs are real. They're not imaginary. And they're not exclusive to me.

If you ask for help, they'll show up. Their energy is still here, always.

Skip was my best friend. Truly. He knew me in ways no one else did. We lived together. We talked every day for eight years. And that bond didn't vanish; it changed form. The energy is still there. It's still accessible.

Recently, I got a call from an ex-boyfriend from before the three husbands. The one who pivoted everything. He was the reason I left academia, the reason I healed my asthma, the reason I shifted into the woman I was meant to become. And now, 22 years later, he called to offer condolences. Another soul thread weaving back in.

In those 22 years? Three husbands. Four careers. Two kids. Massive world travel. Owning homes. Building businesses. Learning, evolving, becoming.

And now I'm talking to my Galactic Family. Channeling my higher selves. Seeing the multidimensional picture more clearly than ever.

So yes, I'm sad. Of course I am. But I also see the beauty in this setup. Skip played his part with perfection. So did CJ. So did Harj. So have Mila and Curran. Everyone gets an Oscar.

I now get to write a new chapter. A new book. One that includes love, yes—but also light, freedom, expansion. Because I'm doing it my way. Not society's. Not grief culture's. Not even his family's.

I've had people tell me I should grieve longer, that I should go to grief groups. But for me, that would be like going to AA or NA and repeating the pain on a loop. That's not how I integrate. That's not how I move energy.

I can talk about what happened, but from different altitudes. I shift. I learn. I tell the story differently as I grow.

So if you're reading this: You get to grieve your own way. There's no right or wrong. And you can connect with your loved ones faster than you think. They are right there. They want to reach you. They love you deeply. Just as I still love Skip. Always.

October 4, 2023—Part 2

I just had this vision, and I love it. Jodie and Sunny are floating above me, sprinkling light dust over me. It's like they've been doing this since the moment of Skip's passing, since this evolution, this death, this transformation, transfiguration … whatever you want to call it.

They're just hovering above me with this playful, sparkly dust, giggling and smiling, joyfully tossing it all over me. And honestly, that's exactly what it feels like. That's been the sensation in my field.

By all accounts, I should probably be deep in grief. I should be sobbing every day, tearing up at everything. But instead? I feel lifted. I feel light. I feel like these two, my fairy godmothers of energy, are up there saying, "Let's keep covering her in it. Let's go!" And it's working.

This is what it means to have amazing friends. Or mentors. Or a soul family.

Sunny especially makes me laugh, because Skip did not want to be read by her. He didn't want to be read by anyone, not by me, not by a psychic, because he knew what he was going through, and he didn't want to be called out on it. Not even a little.

But here's the thing: no one could've changed the trajectory of his life. Feel that. Receive that. Even if you were "the villain," even if you played the "worst" role in someone's story, you were part of their divine setup. And on the other side, they're not judging you. They're thanking you.

So we have to stop judging ourselves. We have to stop overanalyzing what could've been. As I say this out loud, I'm reminding myself too because we are our own best teachers, if we're listening. The answers are inside. Always.

We like to label things: grief, death, awakening. But really, none of those words is quite right. Words carry so much judgment. Use whatever words work for you, and let the rest go.

Love yourself enough to remember: you were born worthy. You were born kind. You were born loving.

No matter what chaos is happening around you—tornadoes, break-downs, societal collapse, global awakenings—there is still peace. In the afterlife, that's what remains: peace. There's no more struggle. It's actually incredibly peaceful and vibrationally rich.

Humans forget that. We get bogged down in "to-do lists," in "I should be doing this" energy. But that's not who we really are.

Some people aren't meant to stay in your life, and that's okay. Some of us signed up to only walk alongside each other for a stretch. So when someone exits your life, even in unexpected ways, it's not always a loss; it's a course correction. Maybe you were meant to brush up against each other, not build a whole future together.

I had that experience recently with friends like Melody and Tom. They were there for me during the fires, like really there. We stayed at their place. And while I don't know if we're meant to stay connected long-term, I'll never forget that gesture. They didn't hesitate. They just said, "Of course."

This island has embraced me. A lot of people feel like the island spits them out. But not me. I've made connections here quickly, deeply. And in this season of life, this strange chapter, I'm surrounded by people who, even if they don't fully get it, are still offering love.

This is my season of transformation. And honestly? I love my island. I feel like I'm giving birth to new islands, like I'm anchoring Earth's renewal. I'm channeling Pelé. And it feels so real.

Now, I'm not someone who can be around just anyone. My energy is sensitive. I feel things. But I also know that in the ultimate realm, of course I can hold space. I came here to do that.

Still, I have my edges. I have my dragon energy. And it's waking up. I haven't fully unleashed her yet, especially in public, but she's here. She's stretching. She's rumbling beneath the surface.

All the dragons are showing up. I feel myself expanding in ways I can't fully explain yet. But I'm growing. And if you're reading (or listening to) this … thank you. Thank you for holding space while I become.

I love Earth so much. It feels like my child. I don't want to give birth to more children; I've done that. But Earth? Earth is one of my creations, and I'm allowed to say that now. I'm allowed to know that.

So now it's my job to help translate what I see. Because if you could see what I see … That's part of why I'm doing this. So you can.

I love you so very much. And Skip, I love you.

CHAPTER 16

FEELING THE LOVE

Here is another voice memo that came through a couple of days later. To summarize:

Watching romantic comedies feels different now. Skip used to love how romantic I was and how much I believed in love. We shared a kind of soul-level connection that went beyond anything I'd known. I still feel him. I miss his physical presence, but the love hasn't left. It's just shifted.

I've come to understand that his sudden departure was part of his soul's plan. Whether we leave slowly or all at once, each path has purpose. What matters is how we live after. I'm choosing to stay open and to keep loving, feeling, and honoring what we had. Because Skip isn't truly gone. He's energy now. And our love still lives.

October 6, 2023

Now, when I watch romantic comedies, it hits differently. Skip used to say that one of the things he loved most about me was how romantic I was, how much I loved the idea of love. I'd watch all the Hallmark Christmas movies, as sappy and predictable as they are. We all know the plot. We all know the ending. But I loved the sweetness, the innocence, the simplicity of it.

I'd invite him to watch with me, well, sometimes I'd more than invite him, but I did it because I wanted him to see the potential of love. Even though it's Earth-based, human love, and different from soul love, it still holds something sacred. It's soft and cute and beautiful. And in many ways, it's pure.

It's not the same as the love you feel for a child, that fierce, primal mama bear energy. Romantic love is different. Especially when you think you've met the love of your life, and then one day you realize, oh wait, I actually did.

Watching these movies now, in the wake of losing Skip, feels tender. There's sadness. There's also hope. A sense that new chapters are possible. A remembering of all those little firsts: The first kiss. The first touch. The first time you make love. And then the first time you really make love when you're no longer nervous, when you know each other's bodies intuitively, when the connection becomes transcendent.

That's where the magic was for us. That soul-level love where just a phrase, a glance, or a single touch could shift the entire atmosphere between us. We had that down to an art.

When I look at the photos, I still have the hots for my husband. Truly. He didn't always know how magnetic he was, how much I loved his body, even when he didn't. For me, it was never about how he looked. It was about how his energy moved through that body. He knew how to use it as an instrument of connection, intimacy, and love.

When our eyes locked in those moments of deep connection, I would see visions, lifetimes. Not just on Earth. I saw us from pure source, creating entire realities together. That happened a week before he died. I had a full vision of who we were, why we came here, and how we were creators, together.

And you reading (or listening to) this? You're a creator too. We're all just pure source energy, choosing experiences. So the real question becomes: what do you want to create?

Skip and I had this dream vision burst out of us. Maybe that's why we didn't have biological children together. We had to find each other later in life. Sometimes when people have kids too early, they get wrapped up in them and lose the connection in their partnership. I've seen it. It doesn't mean that's true for everyone, but it's a pattern I've witnessed.

Other people are here to have multiple partners, multiple families, and more complex soul agreements. That's beautiful too. There's no right or wrong in this. We get so caught up in what other people will think that we forget to ask ourselves: Am I actually enjoying this experience? If not, how do I shift?

Energy doesn't die. It just transforms. So whether you find yourself in a new love, a new career, or even an addiction, whatever path you're on, it's part of the soul journey. Sometimes messy. Always meaningful.

This is what my connection with higher-dimensional beings has taught me. This life? It's a game. A matrix. A soul experiment. We are avatars, and death is part of the rules here. Whether we leave through illness, accident, suicide, or age, it's all a departure plan.

Skip chose a sudden exit. But if he hadn't, I think his soul would've eventually manifested illness to check out. He had been carrying emotional heaviness for years. I sensed it, even had visions of it, long before it happened. I just didn't want to believe it. It still shocks me. But in hindsight, I can see it.

I have friends who've been in the same place with multiple suicide attempts, deep despair, and this inner knowing that they just can't go on. I get it. Earth school is fucking hard.

Some people leave slowly, through illness. My aunt once told me that she believed my grandmother created her ovarian cancer to leave her life. I believe it too.

There's the slow leaving and the sudden leaving. Both are painful. With the sudden, there's no goodbye. No time for closure. But sometimes, that's exactly what the soul needs, to leave swiftly, cleanly, without the entanglement of emotional processing.

I know some people won't agree with this perspective, and that's okay. But from what I've experienced, through my own spiritual journey and the mediums who've connected with Skip, his energy has been transmuted by all the love people sent him. He's in a place of light now. No more pain. He's still with me. And no, he's not even a "he." He's consciousness. Pure energy. Androgynous. Expansive. Beyond gender.

He shows up. I hear bells. I feel the shift in the air.

We are so much more than these bodies. This is just a costume. And when you really know someone's essence, like I did with Skip, the connection doesn't disappear. I miss the physical. Of course I do. I miss his smell. His snuggles. His humor. His dancing. Even his constant pot smoking, which used to annoy me. Now? I'd welcome it. I'd laugh with him and say, "Light up, babe."

If you're still with your person, and you love them, cherish them. Even the little things that get under your skin. Because those are the things you'll remember. Those are the things you'll long for.

I could choose to shut it all off. Be angry. Stay bitter. But I won't. I'm choosing to let the anger dissolve into light, because I understand. When you understand someone's why, it softens the edges. It takes away the charge.

Each day, I feel our connection growing stronger. Not because he's physically here, but because I'm choosing to stay open to the truth that energy never dies.

I love you, Skip. Thank you for choosing me. You are the love of my life. And I know we'll repeat this story in some form. You're already with me.

As Sunny says, the love never ends. And it doesn't.

CHAPTER 17

FIFTY YEARS OF SPIRITUAL PRACTICE

Here is the next transmission that came through via voice memo. To summarize:

When people ask how I'm doing, I tell them the truth. I'm okay. And I mean it. Decades of spiritual practice have prepared me for this moment of moving through grief with a grace that comes from having rebuilt myself over and over. I've faced loss, failure, and reinvention so many times that I trust my own resilience.

Losing Skip is different, though. The love is still here, alive in every cell. I feel him helping me from the other side, guiding the next chapter of my life, curating who and what comes next.

I'm not rushing into anything. I'm savoring this space to be intentional with my days, my work, and my energy. I know the soul never dies, and our relationship hasn't ended; it's simply transformed. Skip is still my partner, my teacher, and my love. I'll keep walking forward with him beside me, in a new form, for the rest of my life.

October 8, 2023

I ran into Anthony, one of Skip's friends, and he asked me how I was doing. I told him the truth. I said, "I'm doing okay." And he just looked at me. Really looked. And said, "I don't know how you're doing it. I can barely hold it together, and it was just a breakup for me (he and his girlfriend had recently broken up)."

I could feel the weight of his sincerity. I didn't have a cute, surface answer. What came out was simple and real: "Fifty years of spiritual practice. That's how."

Because that's what it is. That's how I'm able to do what I'm doing, to move through the grief, the shock, the surrealness, with a sense of grace that might look like strength but is actually the result of decades of living. Not just living, but learning. I've been practicing for this moment my whole life.

I'm about to turn 51. When I zoom out, I see it clearly: I came into this life for a lot. I've had journeys that might look "hard" on the outside. And yeah, some of them were, from the human lens, but they were also soul-designed. Initiations. Invitations. Expansions.

By the time this happened, I had already lived so many lives inside this one. I've had four careers (and I'm only halfway through the fourth). I've had three husbands, or as my friend Kelly wisely calls them, "wasbands." And Skip, he wasn't just another husband. He was the one. My dream. My love. My mirror. My heart.

But here I am again, staring down the next chapter. And somehow, I'm not collapsing because I've already collapsed and rebuilt. Many times.

I've lost everything. Financially. Emotionally. I've declared bankruptcy. I've moved. I've started over. Again. And again. And again.

I've had my identity stripped bare, rebuilt from nothing, reinvented from rubble. I feel like a cat working through her seventh or eighth life, still climbing, still curious, still loving hard.

Even in the devastation of losing Skip, there's something different. It's not like my previous marriages, where I was depleted, resentful, done. With Skip, the love is still here. Still alive. Still glowing in every cell.

I look at his pictures and still have the hots for him. He was my baby. My dream man. The one. And yet, now I'm living in a new dimension of that love.

I trust him to help me from the other side. I've already asked him for things, and he's delivered fast. It's clear. He's part of the source field now. So whether you want to say he did it, I manifested it, or Source moved through us both, it doesn't matter. It happened.

Skip has already promised that he'll help bring the right people into my life moving forward. No more dating losers. No more wasting time with people who aren't equipped to meet me where I'm at. He's still helping me curate the next phase. And no, I'm not ready for that next person yet. I'm really enjoying my alone time. I haven't had much of it in the past. Now, I'm giving myself space to be.

I want my days to be intentional. Purposeful. Soul-led. If I want to start the day at the beach or in meditation or just sipping coffee in the quiet of my courtyard, I want to give myself full permission to do that. And then maybe see a few clients, lead a UFO tour at night, work on the next book, as more books are coming. Skip knows this too. He's part of the creative team now.

While I'm not actively "calling in" anyone new, I know that if and when someone arrives, they'll have to understand that I'm not shrinking to fit any old paradigm again. This, my channeling, my galactic work, my path, is not going away. They'll have to love me as I am. And that's nonnegotiable.

So how am I doing this? Because I've lived through so many cycles already. Because I've learned how to be alone. Because I've built a deep, unshakable foundation of self-trust. Because my mother taught me to be self-sufficient. Fierce. Capable. Because I've faced enough pain to understand that it's not the end.

Even at this moment, widowed at 50, I still feel young. I still feel vibrant. And I still have a deep well of love inside me.

Skip didn't always understand how loved he was. By me. By his friends. By the community. But he was. Deeply. He touched so many people, always the first to help, the first to offer without expectation. That was who he was. That is still who he is, in essence. And while the physical presence is missed, his energy hasn't left. Not even close.

Let me say this clearly for the people on the outside looking in: No, I'm not going to fall apart. No, I'm not going to be destitute. No, I wasn't financially dependent on Skip. That was never the dynamic. So yes, I'm okay. Truly.

I miss him. I love him. I always will. And I know he's guiding me now from a place of joy and clarity that he couldn't always access in human form.

This is how I do it: Because I know this life isn't the whole story. Because I've fallen and risen too many times to believe anything is final. Because I know the soul never dies. Because love never ends. And because this relationship is still happening, just in a new form.

Skip, my love, thank you for being my greatest teacher. I will love you always. And I trust that the next right steps, whatever they are, will come, just like you said they would. Until then, I'll keep walking. I'll keep living. I'll keep loving. And I'll keep listening for your whispers in the wind.

CHAPTER 18

LOVE LIVES WITHIN YOU

Here is the next transmission that came through via voice memo. To summarize:

For me, moving forward with grace begins with remembering that I'm already whole. That truth was alive in me long before Skip, and it's still here now.

Our relationship was never built on need. It was a conscious choice rooted in self-love. Even though his physical form is gone, the energy of our connection remains. I've been through many endings with relationships, careers, and identities. Each one taught me how to rise stronger, clearer, and more embodied.

At 50, I carry the wisdom of all those lives I've lived inside this one. I'm not collapsing. I'm evolving. I know I'll always love Skip, but I also know my life isn't over. There's more joy to come, more expansion, and more becoming. I'll keep meeting each step with open hands, because that's what I came here to do.

October 9, 2023

What's the key to moving on and doing it with grace? For me, it's understanding the love that lives within you. The truth that you are already whole and complete, no matter who is in or no longer in your world.

People will come and go. Sometimes through misunderstandings. Sometimes because the contract is complete. Sometimes through illness or death. But whatever the reason, their absence doesn't erase your worth.

When I first met Skip, I was already on a deep journey of becoming whole within myself. That's what *Sacred Soul Love* was all about. It was about learning to be so at peace with who I am that it didn't matter who came or went. I knew my value. I knew my essence. I loved myself.

When I chose to be with Skip, it was just that, a choice. Not from need. Not from lack. But because I genuinely wanted him in my life. I didn't need him. And that's something we talked about often, especially in the beginning. He appreciated that about me. There was no codependency. No grasping. Just the desire to share love.

Now, even though his physical presence is no longer here, I haven't lost that core truth. I haven't lost my love for myself. I haven't lost my sense of wholeness. If anything, I know it more clearly now than I did when we first came together.

This physical chapter is over, yes. But the relationship itself isn't. The energy remains. It's something I can always access, always tap into.

So, for anyone walking through loss, the work begins by finding that well of love inside yourself. Truly knowing that you are enough. Just as you are. Not because someone else is beside you, but because you are here.

I know some of you have been with your partners for a very long time and haven't experienced the kind of endings or transitions that I've had, boyfriend after boyfriend, three marriages, two divorces. Each time, I rebuilt. Each time, I found myself again.

Those experiences gave me clarity. They taught me that no matter how shattered I might feel, I can rise. I always have. I am a phoenix. And I've risen more than once.

The same is true of my professional life. I've had multiple careers. Each reinvention taught me how to trust myself again, how to move forward with purpose and grace.

So now, at 50 years old, I carry the lived truth of that wisdom. Fifty years of spiritual learning. Fifty years of embodiment. And that's why I'm able to meet this moment the way I am. It might look different than how others move through grief. That's okay.

I'm here to show you that there's another way. You *can* move through it with peace. You can live on with open hands and an open heart.

You are allowed to evolve. You are meant to evolve. That's why we're here on Earth, in these bodies, in these lives. To grow. To deepen. To remember who we are.

We are not these bodies. We are energy. Energy never dies; it only changes form. That understanding brings me peace. Peace in my heart. Peace in my mind.

I know I'm going to be okay. More than okay, actually. That part is already written. It's done. I'm simply walking it out now, step by step, into my expansion, my evolution, my next becoming.

And I will always love Skip. That beautiful man, physically, energetically, spiritually, will always be a part of me. But I also know I will move forward. I will have new experiences. New adventures. New moments of joy.

My life is not over. I'm only 50. There's so much more to explore. So much more to discover. I will continue to grow, to learn, to deepen my connection with Source, with myself, with all that is.

I will stand in my light. I will be light. For myself. For others. And I will continue seeing it all through the higher lens, the one that reminds me why I came here in the first place.

CHAPTER 19

UNDERSTANDING EARTH SCHOOL

Here is the next transmission that came through via voice memo. To summarize:

I understand Earth school. I came here knowing it would be hard, and I said yes anyway. I've spent decades living as a multidimensional being, remembering past and parallel lives, studying soul contracts, and anchoring spiritual truth into everyday human messiness.

That doesn't mean I don't question myself. I do. But I also know I chose this. Every relationship, every loss, every heartbreak. Skip and I planned this love. He helped me experience a kind of self-love I never saw modeled growing up, and now, even after his passing, he's still with me and guiding me. He is still part of me. I've walked through more than most, and I'm still standing and loving. I'm here to hold the light. I truly believe I've crossed a threshold, and what comes next is why I came to Earth in the first place.

October 17, 2023

Here's the thing about being a conscious, fifth-dimensional being, one who remembers past and parallel lives, one who's been immersed in spiritual principles for decades: I get this Earth reality. I understand Earth school.

We came here to ride the roller coasters. To have real, messy, beautiful, challenging experiences. To grow from them. And sometimes that doesn't always land well with others, especially when you're seeing things from a higher perspective. When you understand contracts. When you know you've chosen this. When you feel that bigger picture in your bones, but someone else doesn't. And that's okay.

We came here to model a new way. A new frequency. A new level of presence and perspective. We're here to show others that they don't have to take everything so personally. That we really did set all this up ahead of time. That the love we feel is real because it was orchestrated by us. From before this life. And those we love? They've always been with us. They're still with us now.

So when things feel hard, when I question myself, because I do, I remind myself: I signed up for this. Earth school is hard. But I came here anyway.

I'm here now to help usher in a new reality. To hold light. To live it. And I really hope, truly, that whatever I told my Galactic sisters before coming here, this is it. The final initiation. That I've finally crossed the threshold into blooming. And that the next 50, maybe even 100 years, are spent doing what I came here to do.

I thank Skip every single day for being the one who helped me experience the love I was meant to know. The love I came here to learn because I didn't grow up in a family where self-love was modeled. That wasn't something I was handed. It was something I had to fight to find.

And yes, I've had a string of relationships. That's a whole separate book, or maybe a trilogy of romcoms. The breakups, the drama, the soul contracts. Three marriages. And now? A new chapter. A new era.

I'm not just here to survive. I'm here to *usher in* fifth-dimensional consciousness. To be a lighthouse for what's possible.

I've been through it all: heartbreak, loss, financial ruin, divorce, suicide. The only thing I pray I never have to endure is the loss of my child. I say that because I've already walked to the edge of that cliff with my daughter with three suicide attempts. And with my first husband, I thought he might take his life too. He didn't. But Skip did.

So here I am. Still standing. Still serving. Still loving.

We are here to be the new light. To remember our connection to Source, especially when we feel separate from each other, from our loved ones, from Spirit. But we are not separate. Skip is still with me. He's my soulmate. He is me. He's the mirror of every part of me. When I remember that, when I understand that the part of me that was him chose to exit in such a dramatic way, I can look at it through the lens of soul curiosity.

Why did I choose that? What was I not willing to do, or able to complete, in this physical form? What lesson did that version of me come here to hold, and ultimately surrender?

Earth school isn't easy. It was never meant to be. But we came. We said yes. There are easier realms we could've incarnated into. But we chose Earth. We chose the full ride, the dips, the loops, the climbs, the chaos. But none of that is who we really are. It's just the ride.

So if anything I'm sharing resonates with you, know this: This is my process. My knowing. My decades of spiritual work meeting me at my edge.

I know without a doubt, we are never truly separated. We are all one. All connected.

I love me. I love Skip. And I love you.

CHAPTER 20

ALLOWING THE GRIEF TO BE

Here is the next transmission that came through via voice memo. To summarize:

Some days, the grief feels heavy, like today. I've been noticing how Skip still shows up in songs on Pandora, in the smell of weed on the drive back from Kona, in dragonflies instead of cockroaches, and even in Jaxx's wild bursts of energy. I feel him. I thank him. And I miss him so much.

There are still little things, like the Jeep that won't sell, that hold echoes of our life together. I know I haven't fully let go, and maybe I'm not supposed to yet. I'm grateful for the new spiritual people entering my life and the subtle ways Skip is supporting me from the other side. I know I won't always feel this messy or raw, but right now, I'm still deep in it. Through it all, I keep saying thank you for the love we shared, for his presence now, and for the spark he brought into this world.

November 4, 2023

I pushed you out of your comfort zone with the sharks and all the water activities, and you pushed me out of mine with the motorcycle. That's probably why I haven't even tried to sell it.

The Jeep, I have no real love for. But for some reason, it still hasn't sold. And Dixie, whom I had zero love for, got to go immediately. Maybe there's still something energetically tied up with the Jeep. Maybe I haven't fully released what it holds.

We had good times in that Jeep. Driving with the top off to the ferry, speeding so we wouldn't miss it. So yes, there's still some attachment. And maybe that's why, energetically, it's still here.

I miss you. I love you. Not the "stinky feet" smell, which you only did once, and not the cockroaches. The cockroaches kept coming back. But now … I'm seeing dragonflies. I prefer the dragonflies.

And today, I smelled the pot smell. Yesterday too. I don't know if it was yesterday or the day before, but it happens every day when I'm driving back from Kona. You've been speaking to me through the Pandora station, songs all day long.

So thank you. I know you're still here with me. I'm accepting all the ways you're showing up now. I miss you deeply. I'm still very sad.

I don't like that your brother is still struggling. If there's anything you can do from your side to help him, please do. I know it's not my job to carry that for him.

I love you. Thank you for showing up. For still being here. I know Jaxx has been going wild at times. Thank you for that. I know you're behind some of it.

Thank you for all the new spiritual people who've come into my life. They're all signing up spiritually (the UFO tour), except today's people. So thank you, whatever you're doing from that side. I feel it. I appreciate it.

And I won't always be this much of a mess. I just … I miss you so much. Now we're almost two months into this. Or maybe it's a month and a half. I don't know. Time's blurry. But I miss you.

You brought such a joyous spark and so much love to this world. Thank you for the time I had with you physically. And thank you for still coming to me now. I love you.

CHAPTER 21

DATING AGAIN

In early November, I traveled to Las Vegas for a UFO conference. Skip and I had initially planned to attend together. Instead, my dear friend Cat joined me, flying in a day after I arrived. I took that first night alone as an opportunity to unwind and acclimate, not just to Vegas, but to my new reality.

That evening, I parked myself at a hotel bar to people-watch and soak in the energy. I ended up chatting with the bartender for a while before a young man named PJ sat down next to me. He wanted a better view of the hockey game playing on the TV. We struck up a conversation easily, and I soon learned he was a police officer from Massachusetts, flown in as a "ringer" goalie for a hockey tournament.

Almost immediately, we dove into a deep conversation. I shared that I was recently widowed, and he told me he had just lost his father, possibly to suicide, and that therapy hadn't been helping.

I knew instantly he had been placed on my path for a reason. I shared with him alternative healing methods and spiritual tools that had helped me. He was open and grateful. We spent hours wandering the Luxor Hotel, as if we were characters in one of those dialogue-heavy indie films I love watching.

We met up again the next day before Cat arrived. It was innocent yet intimate, with conversation, laughter, and gentle flirtation. There was no expectation, but it awakened something inside me. It reminded me of the movie *How Stella Got Her Groove Back*. I was Stella because this man was much younger than me. For the first time in a while, I felt alive, desirable, and full of possibility.

By the time the conference began, I walked in with confidence and joy. I was not a grieving widow, but a multidimensional, radiant version of myself. That trip fully initiated me into the UFO world as a professional, and it marked a decisive shift in my energy and purpose.

When I returned to Hawaii, PJ and I stayed in touch sporadically through flirty texts. But more importantly, I had begun reconnecting with myself. With my daughter away on the mainland for Thanksgiving, I found myself in sacred solitude. I made crystal art, hosted a small holiday market at home, and binge-watched every Christmas movie I could find.

That alone time gave me space to reflect. I didn't need anyone to tell me I was ready to date again. I knew it was time to test the waters. I felt emotionally grounded and guided. Skip had already come through in spirit to say to me that romance would help reignite my creativity and joy. So, I took the leap and joined a couple of dating sites, being clear in my profile about my spirituality and galactic interests.

The responses were mixed, as expected, but I did meet some kind, meaningful people, each of whom had also experienced profound personal loss. I could feel Skip's hand in all of it. He was sending me people who needed healing as much as I did. These brief encounters reminded me of my capacity for connection. I wasn't looking to replace Skip. I was exploring what it meant to be open again.

After going on a few dates with various people, I decided to take a short hiatus from dating, as none of them were in complete alignment with what I wanted in my life for a partnership.

When I returned from visiting my mom, Jen, and Chris in Washington over Christmas, I felt a renewed sense of clarity. I immediately joined a different dating app from the ones I tried in November. This time, I created a fully aligned profile that boldly shared my galactic identity. I wasn't here to hide. I was calling in someone who could meet me at my frequency.

That very night, I matched with someone who caught my eye. His profile featured beautiful glass fish art. As a former fish biologist, I was intrigued. I sent a message complimenting his work. This man, Isaiah, would become a significant turning point in my personal and professional life.

I didn't know yet that he already knew who I was. He had briefly met me a couple of years before when Skip and I had started doing the UFO Tours. We used to stand on the corner near our viewing spot with inflatable ETs so that our guests could find us more easily. Isaiah lived in the condos across the street from our corner. One night after work, he stopped to find out what we were doing. I gave him my business card and explained the tour.

The connection was immediate. Isaiah was spiritual, curious, and utterly open to my world. He had been an experiencer of ET activity throughout his life. The next day after matching, I invited him to join one of my spiritual UFO Tours. He said yes.

During the meditation portion of the tour, he had tears in his eyes. He shared how deeply the experience had affected him. He had been in a bit of a funk for a few weeks, and his back was hurting him. After the meditation, he felt lighter and his back didn't hurt anymore.

As we said goodbye after packing the car up with the gear, he offered me tomatoes from his farm, and he gave me a hug that felt electric. I could feel it in my heart.

Later that night, I invited him over for more conversation. He was already in bed when I messaged him, but he felt the pull to come over. After a great conversation, he had to go home and go to bed. When he kissed me goodbye, it was sweet, unexpected, and honest. He even surprised himself.

Isaiah marked the beginning of a new kind of connection. It wasn't about replacing what was lost, but about honoring where I was now. It was the start of something curious and unfolding, just like the next chapter of my life.

CHAPTER 22

VEGAS AND VULNERABILITY

The following few chapters are more voice memos I recorded after my trip to Vegas and my reflections on beginning to meet and date new people. Here is the next transmission that came through via voice memo. To summarize:

With the house quiet and Mila gone, I've been sitting in a lot of emotion. The rom-coms I keep watching bring it all up. I miss Skip. I haven't talked to him in weeks, but I know he's still here. Jaxx won't stop barking at the same corner. The signs are everywhere.

Vegas woke something up in me. The UFO conference felt like home. I felt like me again, alive, connected, and purposeful. I know Skip had a hand in all of it. From the airport announcement of his name, Steven Thompson, to meeting PJ, a 29-year-old cop, who wasn't a long-term match, but helped me feel seen, desired, and human. I know Skip sent him.

I've been drinking more than usual, just trying to stay grounded in a world where I sometimes feel too much. But underneath that is still this deep ache for intimacy, for touch, for connection. Even in the joy of new possibilities and new people, the grief is still here. And so is Skip.

November 21, 2023

So it's been a while since I've talked to you. Mila just flew out today, right before Thanksgiving. And now I've got the house to myself for two full weeks. At first, it felt good. Quiet. Spacious. Like I could finally exhale.

But now I'm here watching all these holiday movies, the kind Mila keeps telling me not to watch because they sometimes involve sadness, or death, or even suicide. She doesn't want me to go there. But I can't help myself.

And Jaxx … he keeps barking at the same corner. I know that when he's barking like that, it's probably you.

I'm sad. I'm really sad. Yes, I have Mila. I have Tanu. I have you, but I haven't talked to you in weeks. It's absurd. I know I've been distant. And yet, somehow, I had an incredible time at the UFO conference. I felt like myself again, back in my element. That energy of collaboration, that's still alive in me. It's not gone. I know it's still there. And I know you were there too.

Vegas. Wow. The moment I stepped off the plane, they were calling out "Steven Thompson, Steven Thompson," and I smiled because I knew that was you. I had asked you to support me, to bring in opportunities, and you did. You really did. You even brought me PJ.

I mean … PJ. Really? Of all people, I meet him in a bar at the Luxor. You set that one up. Not something long-term, not even a real match. But he helped open me up again. I know you did that on purpose. You were always so worried about aging, about staying young, and always complimenting me on how youthful I stayed. So you sent me a 29-year-old? I mean, come on … I'm almost 51. I could be his mom. Seriously.

And he's a cop. A cop, Skip. You know how I feel about cops. But I get it, clearly another lesson. Another mirror. He doesn't even have typical cop energy. He's not aggressive. He's just young. Not super communicative. But what he gave me, what you gave me through him, was the chance to feel beautiful again. To feel wanted. Desired. That mattered.

I'm still laughing that the *Sacred Soul Love* deck literally has a card that says, "You are desirable at any age, any size." And here I am, living it.

Was it love? No. It was Vegas. A connection formed through shared grief. His dad died. You died. That's how we met. So, of course, you orchestrated it. And now I'm left sitting with the ache of that. That romance piece. It doesn't matter how spiritual I am; my human still misses being held.

I'm drinking more than I should. I know that. It's not helping. It lowers my vibration, and I feel it. But part of me thinks I do it to stay grounded, so people don't find me "too much." Because if I stayed in the high frequency I know how to hold, most people just wouldn't get it. Some already don't. And that's okay. They're not meant to. But it's lonely sometimes.

I know you're around. Jaxx won't stop barking. And that woman in Vegas who said she picked up on your energy, maybe she did. Though that snarky side she mentioned didn't quite sound like you. That part didn't resonate. But still, I knew you were with me the whole time.

I loved the connections I made, Tony, especially. That long hug with him, the feeling of being fully seen. No confusion, no weird romantic undertones, just pure, loving soul connection. He's a married gay man. Safe. Real. Loving. That's what I want more of.

I feel like I'm still such a newbie in the UFO world, but it also feels like home. It clicked. I didn't know if it would, but it did. And now there are all these threads unfolding—MJ, Bigfoot projects, Adam, Ian. Who knows what any of it will become? It's all just potential. But I feel alive again in it. I feel like me.

I keep watching my usual rom-coms. It's funny. When I had you here, physically here, I could cry at movies and then just reach over and you'd be there. Now I don't have that. I have to rebuild from scratch.

And Jaxx keeps barking at you. So I know you're here. I do know you're here. I think I'll be ready to let you visit more often soon. It's just me holding back, not you. You're always there. You are me. I am you. We are one. And I'm starting to really get that. Not just conceptually. Deeply.

I love you. Thank you for the magic in Vegas. Stepping off the plane to Steven Thompson. Steven Thompson. Yeah, I'm here alone for two weeks. We'll see what happens. I love you.

CHAPTER 23

THE DAY AFTER THANKSGIVING

Here is the next transmission that came through via voice memo. To summarize:

It's the day after Thanksgiving, and while I tried to keep myself busy with the beach, dinner with friends, and prepping for the vendor pop-up, the heaviness of the season is settling in.

This was one of the strangest, saddest Thanksgivings I've had. I know Skip is still helping from the other side. Vegas reminded me of that, especially through PJ, who gave me a glimpse of feeling desired again.

But now I'm back in the quiet, cleaning the house alone, doing both our parts, and feeling the weight of it all. The dating apps stirred up more sadness than hope. I'm reminded how specific and sacred the next connection has to be. I'm okay being alone, but I don't think I came here to stay alone. Some days I feel like I'm moving forward. Other days, like today, I just miss him and want answers.

November 24, 2023

Okay, so here I am, the day after Thanksgiving. I got to go to the beach at lunchtime, eat poke, and read a book. Then I had dinner with Tina, Frank, Victoria, and her son at Johnny's restaurant, which wasn't my first choice, but it was good to be around people. It was great to see Victoria, and they toasted you. So that part was fine.

But still, this was probably one of the weirdest and saddest Thanksgivings I've had.

In Vegas, you brought me young PJ. I know part of the reason you did that. His dad had just died a few months before. He was alone. I was alone. And maybe you brought him to me to help me see how beautiful I am, even when I don't always feel it.

That weekend felt like a little *Stella Got Her Groove Back* moment. Not just because of PJ, but because of meeting all the people too.

And then there's today. I've been cleaning the lanai and the family room, getting it ready for the vendor pop-up Michelle and I decided to do. The outside work was your part of the house. It's a lot. And now I'm doing the inside and outside. It's a lot to hold. Kind of like with the Halloween party.

I'm feeling a bit overwhelmed. And yeah, I'm sad. I miss you. I didn't want to spend Thanksgiving like this. Christmas is going to be weird too. And our wedding anniversary is coming up. The whole holiday season just feels so different now.

I know you said you were going to bring me people, and I believe you. I'm not trying to be impatient. I'm just curious and want to explore.

Then DA came into the picture, who lives on Maui. We had a great conversation. It was super easy. Spiritually, we had a lot in common.

And then there's JD. Not the one you were jealous of, the other one. I've been thinking about him more and more lately. I don't know if it's just comfort, something familiar, or if there's actually something there. But he's off-island for a few months. We've texted a little.

PJ is super weird with texting. He doesn't want to actually engage, which is fine. I get it.

I was watching one of my dumb Netflix movies, and I opened the dating app, just to see what's out there. Just for fun. I already regret it. It made me cry. It made me message PJ. And it made me want to talk to you. Hence, this memo.

Mila's been gone for almost two weeks, and I thought I'd be okay with that. But I guess just having her energy around, even if she's not home, knowing she's coming back … that's something. That helps.

I know there are people I can reach out to. I'm just not sure who I want to be in the energy of. People are inviting me to things. I just …You know how much I love you.

This whole process has been interesting. Some moments, I feel totally fine, like I'm moving forward. And then moments like this, where I'm just like, what the fuck, dude? Why?

Here's what really hit me: As I was scrolling through that dating app, one I hadn't looked at since right before I met you, I was looking at the photos thinking, *God, I'd so much rather meet someone organically. I don't want to be like some of my other girlfriends, going on dates every night. That might be fun for some people, but I don't have the energy for that.*

And whoever it is, that person is going to be so fucking specific to me. I don't know who they are yet, but I know you told me I wouldn't have to go through losers again, so I'm being protective of my energy.

If it is someone I already know, like JD, then I trust you and my guides will show me signs. I need to be patient. Let him do his process. Let me do mine. Or maybe it's someone new. Maybe it's young PJ. Maybe it's DA from Maui. Maybe someone I haven't met yet.

It's not that I can't be here alone; I can. But I don't think that's what I came here to experience. Today I had a Zoom with MJ, who thinks he's going to be single for the rest of his life … whatever that's about. Anyway, I guess that's all for now. I just needed to talk it out.

CHAPTER 24

CAN SHE JUST GET HER SHIT TOGETHER?

Here is the next transmission that came through via voice memo. To summarize:

Sometimes I joke that if my life were a movie, it'd be called *Can She Just Get Her Shit Together?* And honestly, I'd watch it because the first 50 years have been a wild ride with relationships, reinventions, heartbreak, and healing.

But now I'm in the sequel, writing it as I go. Skip set a high standard for love, but the next person, if there is one, has to be deeply on their spiritual path too. I've been thinking about JD more, feeling the nudges from Skip, sensing the possibilities. Vegas woke something up in me. PJ reminded me I'm still alive, desirable, and capable of deep feeling. Now I'm watching life unfold in real time, holding it all with curiosity. It's this or something better. Either way, I know the next chapter is mine to shape.

November 29, 2023

If this were a movie, this might be the title: *Can She Just Get Her Shit Together?* It would follow the story of the first 50 years, mostly the relationships, but throw in the careers too. Because, let's be real, it's a lot. It would be entertaining. I'd watch that movie. I'd be on the edge of my seat, thinking, *Holy shit. Okay … so what's next?*

Well, here we are now writing the sequel in real time. And it's this or something better. This is the evolution of everything I've created, and it's about to be launched into the stars, into the universe, into the beyond.

Meanwhile, I'm watching my underage daughter navigate her own journey. She's caught up in her stuff, and I know I need to be patient. And with JD, too. I get that if I were to bring him into my world right now, where I'm clearly in charge, he would never fully feel in his power. That dynamic wouldn't serve either of us.

He has to build something on his own. Something solid. Something he feels proud of. Only then could he let someone else into that world … someone like me.

And yeah, I'm doing my part too. Slowing down. Being with the discomfort. Skip set the standard. He gave me love. Support. Passion. Stability. I could rely on him at every moment.

Now the evolution, if there is a "next," is that this person is not only those things but is fully on their spiritual path too. That's the new requirement. That's the new baseline. Because the truth is, spiritual journeys are where things get really hard. People walk together for a while, then diverge. Sometimes they come back together. Sometimes not. But that doesn't make the love or the journey less real.

Skip keeps nudging me toward JD. Not directly, but symbolically. The motorcycle. The signs. The synchronicities. When I was channeling Lisa (my friend in Colorado), I couldn't even remember the exact words, but I remember her delivery. Sarcastic. Sharp. Real. That woman, that soul, is my sister. I love her essence, her edge, the way she mirrors the truth.

So here's where I'm at. I've looked at some of the dating profiles, and yeah, I "liked" a couple of them, but they didn't like me back, which is fine. Honestly, I wouldn't like me either from their perspective. There was no spark. It was all blah. Dating is weird. Online dating? Even weirder.

But Vegas awakened something inside me. It said, Hey, you're still alive. You're still vibrant. PJ showed up out of nowhere, 21 years younger. Twenty-one. But he changed something. He really did. PJ is a game changer, even if it was brief. Even if it was just a moment, he'll always live in a little corner of my heart. What are you doing, dude?

I was talking about PJ with Cat, and she just smiled and said, "So … that was nice." And it was. It reminded me of what I'm capable of feeling.

Then there's JD. Right now, he feels like the evolution of what I had with Skip. Not a replacement. An expansion. Because if Skip were going to pair me with someone, it would be someone who could fully meet me spiritually, emotionally, and intellectually. JD might be that.

And maybe, just maybe, I'll find out he's too much like me. And maybe that's the point. Maybe that's the lesson: to finally meet someone who fully gets me and then see what I do with that.

There's a little sadness that comes with that possibility too. Because everyone really is on their own path. We walk with each other for a time, then we don't. That's just how it goes. And then maybe someone new shows up, steady, aligned, ready to walk beside us again. The potential is endless. I'm learning to hold them all lightly.

Thank goddess I have Jen to talk to about this. I keep reminding myself: It's this or someone better. I don't know where this is going. But the cameras are rolling, and the sequel's being written. One scene at a time.

CHAPTER 25

ECHOES OF OTHER LIFETIMES

W hen I met Isaiah, it felt like a breath of fresh air, a presence I had been longing for without even fully realizing it. He was spiritual, grounded, and multidimensionally aware. We spoke the same language, not just with our words, but through energetic resonance. His experiences with galactic contact mirrored my own, and for the first time in a long time, I didn't feel the need to translate or hold back parts of myself. With him, I could be my full authentic self.

Within days of meeting him, a soul memory surfaced. I remembered us together in another lifetime. It was a sacred union, the kind that transcends vows and lifetimes and logic. That knowing flooded through me with such clarity that I couldn't deny it. He felt familiar, like home, and even though there were clear complications, I chose to stay connected.

At the time, Isaiah was still living with his ex-girlfriend of 18 years. They co-owned a condo and neither of them could afford to move, or so they believed. He was also emotionally preoccupied with another woman, someone he had met months before, who didn't even live on the island. Those things alone should have given me pause. But the bond I felt with him was unlike anything I had experienced. I wanted to see where it could go.

During the eight months we were together as a couple, we created beauty at my house. We transformed my courtyard into a sanctuary. Together, we built a tiki bar, The Milky Way. We extended the pergola and roofed it. We constructed hydroponic garden tables in the exact spot where Skip had taken his life. With his help, I transmuted death into life, pain into peace. That garden became more than a project. It was a portal of rebirth.

In late summer of 2024, we traveled together to Washington to visit his family. It felt meaningful and solid. After the trip, I shared a few pictures on social media, innocently, proudly. But I had forgotten that early on, he had asked me not to post about him. He had personal reasons for that, which I didn't fully understand. I hadn't realized how much that mattered to him until everything changed.

Shortly after we returned from the trip, he ended the romantic part of our relationship. He said he wanted to be just "good friends." The abruptness of it broke me. I had opened my heart fully, believing we were building something lasting. The downgrade in our relationship status hit me like a wave I hadn't seen coming. I agreed to remain friends with him, and we continued as we had been, just without the romance. It was hard!

As I now write this, it's been a year since that change in relationship status. We're still in each other's lives, but not as partners, just good friends, actually best friends. He is building his glass shop in my garage. We're still gardening together. He helps me with my UFO Tours. From the outside, it might look like nothing changed. But inside, everything has.

The mixed signals have continued. Sometimes, Isaiah is tender. Sometimes, he's distant. I've had to learn to hold the ambiguity without collapsing into it. I've tried to date others since our breakup, but no one has come close to the depth of my feelings for him. Still, he remains tethered to his past, entangled with the ex he still lives with.

And yet, something deeper stirs beneath the surface. We have shared many lives together, being part of a soul group. My memories of one of our parallel lives as Uluru and Vael'ryn have only continued to grow stronger—Uluru, my Arcturian self, and Vael'ryn, his Sirian self.

In that lifetime, we shared a sacred love, forged through lifetimes of devotion and service to the Galactic Council. And here we are again, drawn together, but not fully able to unite. There are glimmers of hope that we will.

Recently, Skip came through a medium with a message I didn't know I needed to hear. He told me, "You have to put yourself first. You forgot about you." I had been waiting for Isaiah to choose me, for clarity, for closure. But Skip's words shook something loose.

I remembered who I was. This chapter of my life isn't about waiting for someone else to choose me. It's about choosing myself. It's about returning to the heart of my own mission, not because someone else is walking it with me, but because my soul demands it.

I don't know what the future holds with him. We may still be in a crossing of timelines. Our connection was a catalyst. I hold a profound, soul-level love for Isaiah, regardless of our current relationship status. But I do know this: I will no longer abandon myself for love, not again. That is the deepest, most sacred union of all.

CHAPTER 26

BEGINNING SPARKS OF LOVE

The following is a voice memo, a month and a half after meeting Isaiah. To summarize:

Love and grief move in similar cycles. They are messy, nonlinear, and completely personal. I've learned that real love, the kind that comes after you've done the inner work, is unmistakable when it arrives. I felt that with Skip. I feel it now with Isaiah. The connection is undeniable, but the timing isn't aligned yet, and that's hard. I'm not willing to settle or dim myself while he figures things out, but I also can't deny the truth I feel in every cell of my being. I've seen who we've been across lifetimes. I love him. And I'm holding that love while staying rooted in myself. Because no matter who shows up, or doesn't, I know I'm already whole. I'm the love of my own life. That's the foundation. And from here, only aligned love gets invited in.

February 11, 2024

The stages of a relationship are a lot like the stages of grief. People expect a certain timing. That there's a "right way" to move on. But just like with grief, the timing is different for every person. Yes, healing is part of the journey, but how long that takes, what it looks like, how it unfolds, that's uniquely ours.

If you've ever truly loved someone, not the version of love that's needy or codependent, but the kind that comes after you've done the work, after you've fallen in love with yourself first, then you know. You know what real love feels like. You recognize it the moment it appears again.

It doesn't need to be explained. It just is. And that kind of love? It's rare. And sometimes, it's the hardest kind. Because, like with Skip, and now with Isaiah, I see it. I get it. I know what it is. And yet, I have to be patient with how it shows up in human reality. Because even if I'm ready, they might not be. Maybe they haven't done the same work. Maybe they can't see the full vision yet.

And that's hard. Some people think I should just move on. That if someone doesn't meet me there, they're not worthy. But what they don't understand is, it's not about worth. It's about timing. And when you move at a quantum pace, waiting feels excruciating. I won't lie. It sucks.

But what keeps me steady is the feeling I feel when I'm in his arms. That knowing. That sense of equality. Of recognition. Of love. Maybe he's still in his human experience, dealing with fear, uncertainty, confusion. And I get it. I really do. That doesn't make it easier, but I understand it.

I know what it's like to have loved and been loved deeply. The kind of love I had with Skip was real. It was supportive. It was divine. And when I'm creating something new, that is my baseline. There's no going back to anything less. No sliding into codependency or playing small. I'm whole. I'm healed. I'm in my love frequency.

Yes, I see love in everyone. But that doesn't mean everyone is meant to be mine. Some of the people Skip brought into my life after he passed weren't my people. They were people who had lost someone too. And maybe that was the only thing we had in common—that shared loss.

Eventually, I had to raise the bar again. I set the intention: "Skip ... plus spiritual ... plus galactic."

Then Isaiah showed up. He was a match. He took the bait, so to speak. He bit into the exact energy I put out. And now here we are, still figuring it out. I think he's still questioning why he even bit in the first place. But I know why. I know who he is. I've seen the visions. I've gotten the readings. I feel it in every part of me.

Every time we're together, I want to know more. He thought he had me pegged, thought I was a certain type, with a certain personality, certain limitations. But never, ever underestimate me. Or any of my soul sisters. We didn't come here to be underestimated. We came here to change this world.

Back to Isaiah … I know who he is. I know who we've been. I've felt the connection in every lifetime. And yes, I'm still independent. I'm still whole. I can stand on my own. But I also want to be held. I want love. I want a partnership. My family didn't model that. The strong, independent women in my lineage never remarried. They dated, then gave up, choosing full autonomy. And while that's a valid choice, it's not mine.

I came here to model something else. The union. The balance. Divine Feminine and Divine Masculine, walking together. And I thought that would be Skip. I really did. We even dreamed of leading retreats together. That vision wasn't just mine; it was seen by others too.

But it didn't happen. Then I tried to fit JD into that mold. He had a lot of what I was looking for. But ultimately, it wasn't him either.

Now there's Isaiah. He's still an anomaly. I've told him what I see. He knows. He's felt it too. We've had so many lives together. And yes, I love him. I fucking love him. And he's still in his own process.

That's not easy for someone like me. Or for someone like you, if you're reading this and nodding along. When you know something in your bones, you can't unknow it. When you see someone, really see them, you can't unsee them, even if they're still figuring it out.

After our trip to Volcano, I let him see even more of me. And I love him. It wasn't some storybook weekend. We moved through it. Later, I showed up for him in a different way. It wasn't meant to be a "happy ending," but it was. We're still figuring it out.

There's so much I love about him. Every obstacle we hit reminds me of what I went through with Skip, the slowness, the wondering, the uncertainty about whether we're on the same page.

Maybe that's part of the pattern. Because after all this healing, I know I'm the love of my own life. And everyone who enters my field now is invited into that vibration. Sometimes, that's enough for transformation to happen. But even if it's not, I remain the love of my life. And that matters most.

CHAPTER 27

EARLY EPIPHANY

The following is the next voice memo, a month and a half after meeting Isaiah. To summarize:

Today I had a big realization. Isaiah doesn't fully see his own worth. He's incredible, but he doesn't believe he's enough to stand beside me as an equal. And while I see his brilliance, I know I can't convince him of it. That's something he has to claim for himself. If he does, great. If not, I'll still be okay because it's this or something better.

Even with his human patterns of structure and routine, he keeps showing up, and that matters. I see the love. And today, that energy rippled into everything, like when Mila and I had a breakthrough about how to use the outdoor space. What started as tension turned into vision. Now we're building out the fire pit, the tiki bar, bringing life back into parts of the house I'd let go quiet. Maybe that's what Isaiah is doing too. He's helping reignite the fire in me, the passion, and the possibility. I've been wondering if I still need fire in my life. But now I remember: I am the fire.

February 12, 2024

Today, I had a big epiphany. Isaiah doesn't feel worthy of standing next to me as an equal, not because he isn't, but because he doesn't yet see what he has to offer. He thinks I know more. Feel more. Have more access. But in my experience, that's just not true. He's incredible. Truly. I told him that in the garden, and I meant every word.

But you can't convince someone of their worth. They have to come to it on their own. Either he'll rise into that truth, or he won't. If he doesn't, if he lets me go because of it, I'll be okay. I really will, because it's this or something better.

As we were leaving Volcano (Kilauea) the other day, he spontaneously turned off the main road to drive up to the visitor center (of Mauna Kea). I could tell he was testing the energy, curious how I'd respond to a detour. But I had nowhere else to be. I had blocked the whole day for him, so of course I was in.

His car handled it well. We toured around and stopped at a few spots. I took some photos. On the way down, we started smelling something burning, probably the brakes. He pulled over. I was hungry, so I ate some almonds. He had his cashews. Then we drove the rest of the way down in slow motion.

We came back to my house. And here's the thing, everything he's trying to be, it's not who he truly is. But in this human reality, he is doing the thing. Practical. Structured. Following the rules.

That's not his actual energy, but he's living that way right now.

He dropped me off to go do his chores. Normally, those take all day; I've lived through those days before, but he got them done fast and then came back to be with me. That tells me I'm not just a one-time thing. There's evidence, over and over, that he loves me. He just doesn't know how to express it clearly. But the love is there. So much love.

Today, my daughter tried to convince me to move a pool table into the garage. She was like, "We have the biggest, baddest house in the neighborhood," which … based on her friends, we kind of do. Not in the whole neighborhood, but definitely from her perspective.

She wanted the pool table to go next to the glass studio space, the one I already gave to Isaiah. She was pissed that I gave it to him and not to her. But here's the deal. I'd already agreed. I don't go back on my word.

If I've made a commitment and said, "This is your space," then that's what it is. We planned it, and I honor that. That's how I operate. She thought maybe she could override it or just fit her table in there anyway. I pulled out the tape measure. It didn't work.

Then Isaiah said, "What about outside?" Brilliant idea. I have so much outdoor space that's not being used. So when I offered her that option, everything shifted. Suddenly, she wasn't mad. She was seeing potential.

We started talking about the fire pit, tiki bar, and expanding the lanai space into what I'd always envisioned it to be. I love my outdoor space. I had just gotten complacent. Now, boom, things are happening. We're putting the pool table outside. We're building whatever this tiki bar space becomes. I'll bring back a fire pit.

Yes, I've hesitated. Three years living here, wondering: Do I need fire in my life? But the truth is, I am fire. Still, it gets cold. And it's not even about the warmth, it's about the energy. It's about sitting with it. Watching it. Feeling it. The fire is possibility. Transformation. Now someone's showing up, sparking that in me. Bringing the fire of the house, and of myself, back to life. So thank you.

CHAPTER 28

WHERE MANTIS BEINGS AND MEMORIES MEET

Five months had passed since Skip's death. Time moved strangely in grief, slow and heavy, and then suddenly sped by. On February 12, 2024, I met with my friend Lee, a psychic medium, over Zoom. It wasn't planned far in advance, but the timing felt right. I had shifted. I had survived. And now I was listening for something more profound.

Before he even tuned in entirely, Lee said, "There are Mantis beings with you." Of course, there were. The higher-dimensional Mantis beings had been with me for years, part of my healing lineage and my galactic team. Lee knows this well. He often says I'm the only client he has where the galactics come through in every session. It's become a constant presence when we connect.

Then Skip came through. Lee paused, letting the energy settle. "Skip is showing me that the people closest to him had no idea how deeply he was struggling. You weren't supposed to. He didn't want to burden you."

It wasn't about me. That truth landed with a quiet grace, as it was something that kept coming up in all of the readings. I knew it on some level, but hearing it again, from a source so clear, soothed something old.

"He's saying he led you to Isaiah. He's proud of that. He can support you from the other side now." Then a flash of humor: "He's asking, 'Did I do good with that?'" That was Skip, tender and funny.

Lee smiled. "He's acknowledging the altar you made for him, the Hawaiian flowers. He says thank you. He felt it."

And then, admiration. "Skip's in awe of how you moved the energy after he left. How you didn't get stuck. How you chose to step into a new life."

"Skip said, 'You know how I was always on the fence about your beliefs? I know it's real now.'" Lee added, "He's saying, 'She's doing it. She's really doing it.'"

"Skip says he can help you more from the other side than he ever could while he was here. He knows what he left you with, and he honors how you've carried it."

The conversation widened. Past/parallel lives with Isaiah started surfacing. There was recognition that what was happening now wasn't new; it was a return.

"Skip says he did his homework on this," Lee added. "He says, 'It's nice to see her laughing again.'"

"There's fairy energy around Isaiah," Lee said.

I smiled. "He's a gardener."

Lee nodded. "That makes sense. There's a gentleness about him. It feels safe. Good."

Lee said, "Skip chimed in again: 'I'm proud of myself for him. I'm sorry for everything that happened. Thank you for still thinking of me as healthy. That's how it is over here.'"

He repeated what had been said in previous readings. Not because I didn't hear it the first time, but to make sure I believed it.

The Mantis came forward again. Two of them were standing on either side of me. They had worked with me in healing before, especially on my heart and sacral chakras.

"They have a beautiful energy," Lee said. "They're surrounding you. Supporting. They've been part of your team for a long time."

He paused, then added, "You have a really cool spirit team. And you're receiving downloads from the Mantis, ancient wisdom, a different kind of language. They speak in codes, in pulses, like a heartbeat mixed with geometry."

He was right. One night, I'd fallen asleep in Isaiah's arms, speaking in a language that wasn't Earth-based. It was something galactic, something remembered.

"If you open to your Mantis light language," Lee said, "there's an activation waiting. And it's not just for you, it's for others too. You're meant to teach from this frequency."

He added that my team is happy I'm moving forward and wants me to continue to work with my Lemurian quartz and to keep healing.

Skip returned, gently, one more time. "He supports all the decisions you're making. He knows how many times you've cleared the house. It feels better now. He says, 'She turned it into light.'"

And finally, Lee shared one last message: "If you ever wanted to help people move through grief, that would be a very strong path for you. If you choose it. He says, 'You've walked it. You understand it. And you didn't drown in it.'"

The message wasn't a push. It was a quiet invitation. Grief doesn't end. But it does shift. And Skip had become one of the silent forces guiding me forward.

CHAPTER 29

A DEEPER REMEMBRANCE

In November 2024, I was a speaker at an ET Diplomacy conference. This event brought together contactees, experiencers, and those working to build bridges between humanity and our galactic family.

That gathering opened up many timelines for me. Still, one of the most unexpected gifts came through afterward, when I was invited to be a guest on the *Twillow Talk* podcast, hosted by two women, Jen and Tanys.

They knew very little about me before the show. I thought we were going to have a conversation about galactic contact, healing, and consciousness, but midway through our recording, Jen paused and asked, "Are you Arcturian? And a healer?"

"Yes," I replied, curious where she was going with this. She looked at me intently. "I wrote about you in my book." Jen had recently written a book about her memories of being a Lyran during the time of the Orion Wars.

She hadn't published the book yet, but she sent me a copy of the manuscript that same day. As I began reading, chills washed over my entire body. There, in the pages of her story, was a character named Uluru, described exactly as I know myself in that dimension: a Master Healer,

Arcturian, blue-skinned, calm yet strong, carrying wisdom from across the stars.

I am Uluru. I've known this. But to see myself so clearly reflected in a story written by someone I had just met without her knowing anything about my galactic history was a moment of profound recognition and embodiment. It was like receiving confirmation from the cosmos itself.

A few weeks later, I felt guided to show Jen and Tanys a photo of Isaiah. I held no expectations, just an open heart. Jen took one look at the image and said, "That's Vael'ryn." I didn't need any further convincing. I felt it too. A full-body yes rippled through me.

Vael'ryn was Uluru's soul partner in that lifetime. He was a Sirian commander, powerful yet tender, who stood beside her in both battle and peacekeeping missions during the Orion Wars. He was her protector. He was her love.

I had already remembered parts of that sacred connection. But hearing Jen name him so clearly, and seeing how he embodied those identical energetic signatures in this lifetime, deepened my remembrance even more.

I shared the book with Isaiah, and he's now read it multiple times. He continues to express the deep emotions he feels every time he reads it. Though he doesn't consciously recall that life, something has stirred inside him. It's a resonance. It's a knowing without memory.

Soon after, I did a regression hypnosis session with Jen and Tanys to explore that lifetime further. More scenes unfolded, featuring moments of healing, war, and deep trust and intimacy between Uluru and Vael'ryn. Their connection wasn't fast-burning or dramatic. It was earned through shared purpose and aligned frequency.

While that soul remembrance has been a gift, it's also brought its own kind of heartache. Because even with the depth of that connection, Isaiah is still not fully available in this life. He's still living with his ex-girlfriend. Our status has been "good friends" for over a year now, even though the energy between us often feels like something much more.

In May 2025, Skip came through again during a mediumship session and told me, with love and clarity, "You need to stop waiting. You've forgotten yourself. Put yourself first." That message hit me right in the center of my chest. It was the loving nudge I didn't know I still needed.

I shared what Skip had said with Isaiah, and he agreed. He told me I should put myself first. And so I am.

I'm letting the story of Uluru and Vael'ryn be what it was, sacred, real, and complete in its own dimension. I'm no longer trying to recreate it here. If something similar is meant to unfold in this timeline, it will. But only if it aligns with my highest good, without compromising my sovereignty.

I'm open to divine partnership, whether that's with Isaiah or someone else, but I'm not waiting. Remembering who I am means honoring myself first. That is the most potent form of love I can choose right now.

CHAPTER 30

TAKE THE TRIP

If Skip were still alive, I wouldn't have gone to Egypt in 2024. Not because I didn't want to, but because he would've been worried about money, and I was already going to Bali a couple of months after the Egypt trip. That was one of the tensions in our relationship. I could see the abundance around us. He often couldn't.

After his passing, something shifted. Life was no longer something I could take for granted. I could no longer delay the callings of my soul.

A few years earlier, during a QHHT session, I had remembered a life in Egypt, but I wasn't human. I was a Sirian genetic engineer, assisting in the construction of the pyramids and the elevation of human consciousness.

That memory had stayed with me, alive in my body, waiting for a moment to reawaken. I knew I had come to Earth in this lifetime to experience Egypt as a human, and now, finally, I was going.

I heard Skip's voice in spirit saying clearly, *"Take the trip."* It wasn't just about getting on a plane. It was about claiming the next version of myself. It was saying yes to the mission, yes to joy, and yes to the full expression of life, even while navigating the immense sorrow of loss.

Egypt was not a sightseeing trip. It was an initiation. The temples called to me. The stones remembered me. And I remembered them. The vibration of the land, the codes in the architecture, the ceremonies woven into every chamber, all opened something within me. My Arcturian and Sirian selves became more embodied. My multidimensional awareness expanded. My role as a galactic ambassador deepened.

Then came Bali two months later, a sacred container for integration. It was a mother-daughter rite of passage for me and Mila and for Jen and Kylie. The magic of Bali allowed my heart to feel again in all directions, including grief, joy, beauty, and connection.

Both trips felt like something Skip helped orchestrate from the other side. He knew I needed those activations. I needed to remember who I truly was, not just as a widow, not just as a healer, but as a multidimensional being on a mission.

So if you're ever hesitating because of fear, finances, or someone else's limitations, I'll echo Skip's words to me. Take the trip. Let the world initiate you. Let your soul lead. Let yourself live.

CHAPTER 31

GALACTIC EMBODIMENT AND THE SPACE BETWEEN

After Egypt, something permanent shifted in my field. The grief didn't disappear, but it alchemized. I was no longer just moving through pain. I was becoming the person I had always been destined to be. The loss had broken me open. And through that opening, my Galactic Team poured in with clarity, power, and purpose.

I began to channel more consistently and with greater precision. The Arcturians returned with their crystalline healing frequencies. The Sirians brought in structural clarity and galactic memory. The Mantis amplified the energetic threads between dimensions, weaving them into my voice, my hands, and my work.

For the first time, I felt fully embodied as a Galactic Ambassador, not just someone who taught about contact or led starseed retreats, but someone who was the message. I was someone who lived it.

The energetic space that opened after the shift in my relationship status with Isaiah gave me the clarity and stillness to write the book I had been waiting to create: *Awakening to Your Multidimensional Self.*

This book was a soul transmission. It's a blueprint. It's a guide for understanding our true nature. We are not just human beings on a linear path, but multidimensional souls navigating a quantum reality. All timelines exist simultaneously. Every choice we make and every frequency we hold influences the reality we step into next.

Writing it helped me solidify that truth, both as a teacher and a living embodiment of my own multidimensionality. I could feel the echoes of my galactic lifetimes weaving through the pages. The Arcturian. The Sirian. The Mantis. And all of the other lives I had remembered. The ones still waiting to be reclaimed.

The more I wrote, the more I remembered. And the more I remembered, the more I activated. This was an expansion. It was a return to wholeness. I knew, with every cell of my being, that Skip's passing had catalyzed this. His soul, so loving, loyal, and deeply intertwined with mine, had given me the greatest gift. The space to become who I truly am.

CHAPTER 32

STEPPING FULLY INTO MY MISSION

After birthing *Awakening to Your Multidimensional Self* in January 2025, I felt something click into place, like I had recharged at the soul level. It wasn't just about finishing a book. It was about stepping out of the shadows and fully embracing who I am: a Galactic Ambassador, a channel, a bridge between worlds.

With renewed energy and clarity, I knew it was time to take my spiritual and galactic business to the next level. I was no longer afraid of being seen. I was ready to be visible. I was prepared to lead.

That's when I hired my high-end business coach, Alysa. She wasn't just a strategist. She was also a psychic and healer. She had grown her own seven-figure spiritual business, and I felt aligned with her ability to hold both structure and soul.

I would never have made this kind of investment if Skip were still alive. His concerns about money were very real, and I honored them during our time together. But now, I could move in a way that felt expansive instead of cautious. I could say yes to myself fully.

Working with my coach has helped me embody my galactic aspects even more deeply, both conceptually and energetically. She's reflected back to me the magnitude of what I carry, including the resonance and the transmission. She's helping me walk with even more confidence, power, and clarity.

I am fully on my mission now. My role is to share the empowered messages of love and unity, and to help humanity remember who we are and who we've always been. I am here to support the bridging of worlds as open contact edges closer in our collective future. It's no longer a far-off vision. It's a coming reality.

Part of that reality is showing people that death isn't the end. The connection with a loved one doesn't disappear when they leave their body. It simply changes form. Skip is more present in my life now than he ever was in his final months. He supports me in the background, through energy, messages, synchronicities, and unconditional love.

Souls don't die. Only the costume does. I'm here to show what's possible on the other side of loss. This isn't about bypassing grief, but about walking hand in hand with it toward expansion. Healing doesn't mean going back to who you were. It means becoming who you're here to be.

CHAPTER 33

MESSAGES THROUGH THE VEIL

It began before the mediumship reading even started. In May 2025, Lisa Williams sat with a pounding headache, one she suspected wasn't hers. "I have a funny feeling it has to do with our next guest," she said, moments before connecting. I was a guest on her podcast, where she was doing a mediumship reading for me. The headache, as it turned out, belonged to Skip. "I feel like a man is responsible. I know nothing else about it."

When she opened the field, he came through immediately. She described a man close in age, not blood-related, but deeply connected to me. Head trauma. Mental health issues. A sense of internal weight that had lasted for years. Then came the confirmation. "He actually just said that he took matters into his own hands," Lisa said, "and he's letting me know that he is responsible for his own passing."

He had waited for me to be gone, hosting a retreat, because, in his words, "Life had become too hard for me to deal with." Lisa shared that he considered backing out, but knew the pain would only resurface. "This was truly his decision," she said, gently but clearly.

And then: "He's so sorry."

139

Skip showed Lisa the dynamic between us: I had carried so much. I had, in his words, saved him many times. But by the end, he felt like another child to me. "You deserved more than that," he said. "I didn't do it for you. I did it for me."

He said something else I already knew but still needed to hear: "You had no impact on this. This was not your fault."

Lisa described him as deeply spiritual now, which he hadn't been in life. "He said, 'Now I know that there are bigger things.'" He knew I'd felt him since his passing, seen him, spoken to him, sensed him. And he had watched everything. "He's so proud of you," she said. "You've made a success out of your life, and he's witnessed that."

When the conversation turned to my current relationship status of "it's a complicated one," he didn't hold back. "Always put yourself first," he said. "You forgot." Then, with a bit of humor in the pain: "Don't take any shit."

Lisa paused. "Is your mom also on the other side?" she asked. I nodded.

"She just said it was all very much a shock." My mother came in, acknowledging the complex relationship we had. She took responsibility for her part. "She's making me aware that it wasn't an easy relationship … and she tells me that this was a lot of her doing."

She added something I had never heard from her in life. "I'm sorry."

She also spoke of the time after Skip's death and her regret for not being more emotionally present for me. "She felt like she'd let you down," Lisa said. Then a moment of reconciliation came through between them, my mother and Skip. "They've made their amends."

Skip said, "While we had our issues, I never stopped loving you." He acknowledged that I had been exhausted. "You felt very tired, you felt isolated, you were tired of the whole situation." Then came the image of our June wedding. "He makes me aware that it was tiny," Lisa said. "He said you were the most beautiful bride … so casual, so locked in."

Lisa asked if I'd been estranged from my dad. "He's showing me there was an issue with your dad," she said, and then my mother chimed in again. "Your dad's a child," she said bluntly. "He's always been the same. He'll never change."

Then the conversation turned toward my work. Skip showed Lisa the business I've built, the creativity I've embodied, and the women I support. "You can turn your hand to anything," he said. "You've always been able to make money." But he hadn't. Money was a struggle for him, something he said he never quite understood.

He made light of it now. Lisa laughed: "He's joking about how you can make the big bucks, and he can only give you a quarter."

But then he turned serious again. "Look at how far you've come," he said. He showed Lisa my spiritual capacity, which he said had expanded dramatically since his passing. "You've opened up in a major way."

He confirmed that my home was becoming a retreat space, and he supported it. "He said he supports you in this," Lisa told me. "Whatever you're doing with your home, it's right." He saw my growth, the transformation of my life into a sacred offering. "You're going to be channeling the light beings," she said. "The Arcturians, the Pleiadians, the others."

Then Lisa paused. "I've got chills," she said. "Oh boy. This is really big."

Skip said I have "the Midas touch." That my retreats will outgrow my home. That I might even do retreats in places like Alaska. That I'll keep expanding. "Whatever you touch works," he said.

Lisa then asked me about beads and jewelry. "You need to be selling these," she said. "He showed me the beads. They have energy. They're channeled. It doesn't matter how weird it is (the work that you do), people will be ready."

Then came the message from my light beings. Lisa said, "There's something about your connection to them getting bigger. You're going to be healing with them in a much larger space."

Then came the teaching. The truth wrapped in love, delivered through pain. "He said, 'I know I broke you,'" Lisa told me. "But you are not broken. And now it's time for you to rescue yourself."

He warned me not to wait on someone who isn't ready. "You could be waiting longer than you realize," he said, referring to the one I'd been holding space for. "Put yourself first. Take action."

Lisa asked if I was writing a book. I told her I write books all the time. "Finish it," Skip said. "Make it healing. Make it yours."

Finally, he spoke of my son. Though not his biological child, he offered love and acknowledgment. "He wants to give a lot of love to your son," Lisa said. "It's really important that he knows he's still remembered."

He mentioned the tattoo we shared. "I see the tattoo," Lisa said. "He says when you look at it, you think of him."

And then his closing words: "I loved her more than anything. I'll always be the bright star in the sky she sees. I may not be in the physical, but I've got her. I've got her."

What he left behind was grief. What he gave me, what he still gives me, is the strength to live from the truth of who I am.

CHAPTER 34

THE KNIGHT, THE EMPEROR, AND THE THRESHOLD

Cathy, who had done the very first reading for me after Skip's passing, was now, almost two years later, doing a reading for me in July of 2025. She tuned into the energy immediately.

"Alright, so let's see what we've got here. We'll start with the energies around Isaiah ... it can be something where either there's an activation in him or in you ... Maybe it can be that things shift."

She made it clear I wasn't losing myself in this connection. "You're very abundant," she said. "You know how to hold your own energy. Whether he gives to you or not, you're gonna be fine."

She said that being in his space didn't drain me, but it also didn't grow me. Cathy pointed to my solar plexus, saying it had been too closed off, and that being in the "friend zone" with him might have actually helped me strengthen it again. "It's like nobody's going to be vampiric with me. I'm going to maintain my stability."

When she dropped into our past/parallel-life connections, she called him "soul family." We'd played many roles in other lifetimes, even siblings once, but she felt a soft blue energy in the throat chakra. "There was a loving, soft connection in lifetimes."

Now, though, there was indecision. And a refusal to go deeper. "He's been slow in making decisions," Cathy said. "But it's not just indecision. He needs to get to the root of why he can't commit."

She emphasized that it wasn't about other people. "It's about him. He has to heal." Despite that, there was potential. "There is a wish fulfillment potential here. Like the perfect match . . . if a few things click into place." But she paused and added: "And that's a big if."

The foundation, the friendship, the creative spark, and the emotional bond were there. But she warned me about the loop. "You could get worn out from him. Yes, no, yes, no." His emotional withdrawal wasn't just present-life patterning. "That's lifetime stuff."

And his ex? Cathy confirmed she was still watching me. "She's stalking you (on social media). She doesn't have much to give . . . but she's hanging on to this old energetic tassel, and it's keeping things murky."

That energy, the spying, wasn't harmless. "It's not even real anymore. She's holding onto an illusion. But it needs to be transmuted."

Cathy saw clearly how he viewed me: "You're not average. You take up space, spiritual, energetic, leadership space. He knows he'd have to rise into Emperor energy to meet you. But he's not there yet."

Then she said something that hit both of us. "He wants to be your Emperor, but he's still showing up as the knight. The knight can rescue the day one time ... but then the knight moves on."

And that's when she saw someone else coming in.

Enter the Emperor

"There's another man entering the picture," Cathy said. "And he's already the Emperor."

She described someone financially established. "He's mature. Been there, done that. And it left him empty. Now he's looking for real."

She said I'd feel deeply appreciated by him in a new way. "He's going to exalt you. See you as a goddess. He wants someone independent, someone who's doing her own thing. That's you."

His energy felt stable. Solid. Different. "He could be a little too material-focused," she said, "but that's why you're coming in. To show him another side." She described it as a "cat and dog" dynamic, different, but balanced. He would bring tools. I would bring light.

"There's big growth here. You'll grow through this relationship. And he's serious, like come-hell-or-high-water energy. He's determined to win you over."

And unlike Isaiah, this man was ready. "You don't have to teach him how to show up. He just does."

But this connection came with its own warning. "He has an ex too," Cathy said. "She's dark. Sex magic. Jezebel archetype. Very manipulative. She could be doing reckless magic to stay attached. She sees you as the opposition. She's hostile, even cursing you energetically."

Cathy was clear that it likely wouldn't land, but I'd need to stay on top of my spiritual hygiene. "She's trying to tiptoe around, but it's not subtle. She's an elephant in a china shop. And she's jealous, because he sees you as a rising star."

Still, this man was no fool. "He's not going back. That relationship was karmic. He's done. She may try to stir things up, but you're a breath of fresh air to him. It's a whole new frequency."

Cathy said I'd meet him soon. "You're going to have butterflies. And he's going to be ready to build something sacred, maybe not with a contract at first, but with real commitment." And Isaiah? He'd feel it immediately.

What Happens When the Emperor Arrives

Cathy said, "Isaiah will realize he's about to lose you, and not because you wanted someone with more money, but because someone else simply showed up for you."

She described him going from Knight of Pentacles (the slowest moving knight) to Knight of Swords, lightning fast. But that urgency didn't guarantee depth. "He'll try to rush in, passionate, dramatic, full of promises he can't quite deliver." Or can he?

She saw me wanting to say YES to both men for different reasons. She warned that if I tried to juggle both men, it would eventually create conflict. "You'll try to keep Isaiah as a friend, but the new man won't like that. And frankly, neither will your spirit."

In the end, Cathy said I might choose to walk away from Isaiah. Not out of anger. Not out of rejection. But because I had crossed a threshold.

"You're someone special," she said. "And once you feel what it's like to be loved in your fullness, you're not going back for scraps."

Then the focus of the reading turned to my business.

Business, Breakthrough, and the Threshold of Ease

"Your spiritual strength is peaking," Cathy said. "This is your launch point." She described a portal opening, the kind you step through when you've done the work and finally reached the edge of a new timeline.

"You've built your foundation. You're not striving anymore. You're receiving." She saw communication expansion, interviews, shows, and possibly even the *Today Show*. "This isn't small-time anymore," she said. "You're being backed by something big. And the world is ready."

I asked about moving, as Lisa Williams had mentioned seeing me move a couple of months before. She said I would be moving as well. "You'll keep a home in Hawaii, but your main residence is shifting." The Emperor was tied into that too. "He may want you to move in with him. And he's stable."

What I'm seeing now is that none of these threads stands alone. Skip's death opened the portal. Isaiah's energy tests my boundaries. The Emperor arrives as a mirror of what I've become ready for. Is it a new Emperor, or does Isaiah step up to his Emperor potential that Cathy saw in a reading I did with her in January of 2024?

Every choice I make now matters, not because I'll mess it up, but because I'm finally aligned enough that the next step will meet me the moment I take it. This isn't about love or work or location. It's about choosing the version of me that all of this has been trying to wake up.

CHAPTER 35

BECOMING THE ONE
I WAS WAITING FOR

If there's one thing I know now, it's that we never really lose anyone, not in the ways that matter. Skip's death shattered my world. But it also did something else. It forced me to stop straddling timelines and to stop living part in the past and part in the maybe. It asked me to root myself fully in the now, where I am alive, awake, and holding the torch of everything we once dreamed together.

For a long time, I wrestled with the questions most people are afraid to ask out loud. Why would someone so deeply loved leave? What does it mean for their soul and for mine? Did I miss something? Could I have stopped it?

What I understand now, from a higher perspective, is that Skip's soul made a choice, not a mistake, but rather a catalyst. It was one we didn't fully grasp at the time, but one we agreed to before either of us ever came to Earth. His departure wasn't the end of our story. It was the ignition point for me.

The shockwave of his passing moved through every layer of me—physical, emotional, and spiritual. It's that very rupture that propelled me into fuller embodiment. I didn't just become a galactic ambassador. I remembered I already was. I'm a healer, a truth-teller, and a guide, not just for others, but for myself too.

Death isn't the opposite of life. It's a doorway between forms. While I still grieve how he left, I don't question that he's still with me. He isn't here as a ghost of who he was, but rather as part of the foundation of what I'm building.

In every intuitive nudge and every contact with spirit, I feel his presence. It's gently guiding me forward. I've made peace with the truth that I may never fully understand all the reasons. I don't need to. The lesson is in the unfolding.

There comes a moment, after the waves have crashed and receded, when you find yourself standing in the quiet. You're not in the beginning and not in the end, but in the space between. That's where I've been.

After walking through the fire of grief, rebirth, remembrance, and reclamation, I've emerged different. I'm not fixed or untouched, but whole in a new way. There is no going back to who I was before. That version of me no longer exists. And truthfully, she was never meant to stay.

This space I'm in now is not the absence of pain or loss. It's the presence of everything, grief and joy, expansion and uncertainty, human ache and galactic memory. It all lives here together. I've stopped trying to sort it into neat compartments.

In this space, I've come to realize that grief doesn't end. It changes shape. It teaches. It initiates. It carves open parts of us that were sealed shut. It reminds us that love isn't linear, and the soul never dies.

When it comes to love now, I'm no longer trying to recreate what was. I'm not looking to replace or repeat. I'm allowing something new to meet me at the level I now occupy. I continue to clear anything that no longer aligns.

The experience with Isaiah taught me a lot about soul bonds, karmic loops, and the difference between love and readiness and between potential and partnership. It helped me refine my discernment.

In doing so, it prepared me for a different kind of connection. One that is built on presence, clarity, and a shared future. It showed me that I have the ability to love someone other than Skip at a deep soul level.

I don't know precisely what that future looks like. I don't know who will walk beside me in the long run, or where I'll ultimately land. But I do know this. I am on my path. My mission is no longer something I talk about. It's something I live.

The business is expanding. My gifts are sharpening. Opportunities aren't something I chase. They arrive because I've become the version of me they were always meant for.

Timeline shifting is not a metaphor. I've felt it. I've lived it. One life ended when Skip left. Another began the moment I said yes to the frequency of who I'm genuinely here to be.

There's still grief and the ache, but there's also grace. There's momentum. There's a knowing, quiet and unshakable. I'm held by something bigger, and finally, I'm holding myself. This isn't the end of the story. It's the threshold. And I'm walking through it, open, transparent, and ready.

CHAPTER 36

LETTERS ACROSS THE VEIL

Sometimes the words that need to be said the most are the ones that live in our hearts long after the moment has passed. These letters are my way of honoring love in all its forms: earthly, cosmic, and eternal.

To Skip

Babe,

There are still moments when I wake up thinking you're just in the other room. I still hear your laugh sometimes when I'm in the car, or feel your hand brush mine as I sit on the sectional where we used to watch TV and hold hands.

You were my partner, my teammate, my goofy, loyal, brilliant love. We made each other better, even in the complex parts. I wish you had known how much your presence mattered and how loved you truly were, even in the moments you felt lost.

I see now that your soul needed to go. This departure was part of a larger orchestration to set both of us free. And as painful as it's been, I honor that. I honor you. I carry your essence with me every day.

Thank you for showing me what real love looks like. Thank you for being the mirror that helped me see what I needed to heal. And thank you for still showing up for me from the other side with signs, love, and guidance.

Our relationship didn't end. It just changed form. I will love you always.

To Isaiah

My dear friend and mirror,

Meeting you unearthed something in me I didn't know was still waiting to be revealed. You arrived in my life with a frequency I had yearned for, spiritual, galactic, and aligned. We shared a language I didn't have to translate. You carried a presence I already knew.

From the beginning, I remembered you, not just in this life, but beyond. Sacred union. Parallel timelines. Soul recognition. I have no regrets about loving you. Even though we've had to walk the path in ways I never imagined, I am grateful for every step.

You helped me alchemize grief into purpose. You reminded me that love doesn't always look like we want it to, but it still transforms us. Whether we continue to walk together in this lifetime or not, I trust the divine unfolding.

Thank you for being part of my story. Thank you for being who you are. And thank you for showing me that I am worthy of love that feels like home.

May we both keep walking in truth and integrity with hearts wide open. I love you always.

To My Galactic Team

Beloved family of light,

You have walked with me through it all. Even when I forgot, even when I doubted, even when I collapsed in sorrow, you never left.

You reminded me of who I am when I felt shattered. You whispered to me in dreams, sent symbols through nature, orchestrated synchronicities that led me back to my truth. You showed me that death is not an end, and my mission is far from over.

Thank you for trusting me to be a bridge. Thank you for waiting until I was ready to fully remember. I am here now. Embodied. Aligned. Willing.

Let's continue the work. Let's anchor the codes. Let's prepare the hearts. Let's build the bridges between worlds.

I vow to serve with love, to walk in truth, and to stay sovereign. And to always remember … I am not alone. I never was.

To My Divine Partner

To the one who meets me in my fullness,

Thank you for seeing me, not as someone to fix or figure out, but as someone to witness, to walk beside, to cherish. You arrive not as a rescuer or replacement, but as a sovereign soul who chooses me and is chosen in return.

I have journeyed through grief and remembrance. I have sat in silence with ghosts and danced in gardens built on loss. I know now that I don't need a partnership to be whole, but the right partnership can be a sanctuary for the soul.

With you, I want to co-create something rooted in trust and truth. I enjoy laughter, depth, play, and expansion. I want to be held in my softness, honored in my strength, and met fully in all the dimensions I walk in.

I have loved before. Deeply. And I still do. But my heart has room for more. If you are the one aligned with this chapter of my life, I welcome you with grace and gratitude.

Let our connection be sacred, sovereign, and free.

To Myself

Dearest me,

You made it through the impossible. You stood in the fire of grief and didn't burn. You transmuted. You walked through sorrow and still found space to love, to hope, and to create. You chose life again. And again. And again.

There were moments you forgot your light, but you remembered. You always remembered. You listened to the whispers of the trees, the pull of the stars, the hum of your own soul calling you forward.

I am so proud of you. You didn't just survive. You became. You wrote your story in the ink of courage and the language of remembrance. You let your heart stay open, even when it would've been easier to close.

Keep going. Keep loving. Keep trusting. This life, in all its mess and magnificence, is yours. And you are more radiant, more multidimensional, more you than ever before.

To the One Who is Grieving

Dear beautiful soul,

If you're holding this book in your hands, it means you've loved deeply and lost deeply too. Maybe your grief is fresh, raw, and disorienting. It may linger quietly, showing up in waves when you least expect it. However it's showing up for you, I want you to know this. You are not alone.

I see you. I know the way your breath can catch for no reason. The way the world keeps moving like nothing happened, even though everything inside you has changed. I know how surreal it feels to smile in one moment and sob in the next. I know how hard it is to explain what can't be explained.

Grief isn't linear. It doesn't follow the rules. It shows up like ocean tides, some days crashing, other days lapping gently at the edges of your heart. And in that ocean, it can feel like you're drowning. But even here, even now, there is something deeper holding you.

Your love didn't die. It just changed form. You're allowed to miss them. To rage. To feel numb. To laugh too loudly. To start over. To not know what comes next. You're allowed to be every version of yourself in this process. There is no timeline. There is no perfect way to do this. There is only your way, and that is sacred.

I want you to know something else too. You are not broken. This pain isn't proof that you've failed. It's proof that you have loved. And that love, that soul bond, that connection, it still exists even if you can't see it. Even if you're doubting it right now, it's there. On the breeze. In the dreams. In the quiet nudges that remind you to keep going.

You don't have to rush to be okay. You don't have to find silver linings right away. But I promise you this, your heart will grow around the grief. You will find moments of peace again. Of joy. Of meaning.

Let yourself feel. Let yourself rest. Let yourself be held by your guides, your loved ones, and your higher self. This chapter of your life is not the end of your story. Something new will rise from this. You will rise from this.

And when you do, you'll carry more light than you ever thought possible. Not because the pain disappeared, but because you alchemized it into something beautiful. You are more resilient than you know, more loved than you realize, and never, ever alone.

SECTION 2

Finding Your Way Through Grief and Awakening

"We think that the point is to pass the test or overcome the problem, but the truth is that things don't really get solved. They come together and they fall apart. Then they come together again and fall apart again. It's just like that. The healing comes from letting there be room for all of this to happen: room for grief, for relief, for misery, for joy."

–Pema Chodron

CHAPTER 37

PARENTING THROUGH GRIEF

When you lose someone you love, everything in your world rearranges. But when you're a parent, your grief doesn't get to exist in a vacuum. It walks beside the responsibilities, the check-ins, the doctor appointments, and the grocery lists. It seeps into the spaces between mothering and mourning. And somehow, you learn to carry both.

Mila and Curran have walked this journey with me in their own unique ways. Mila stayed close by in distance, but emotionally, she kept her space. She didn't want to be in the house after Skip died. The energy was too heavy for her. It was too overwhelming. She spent most of her time elsewhere, which I understood.

I didn't push. I did my best to support her as she continued in therapy, working through her own grief in a way that made sense for her. While I know I did what I could at the time, if I'm honest, there were moments I could have been more present and more emotionally available. However, I was still learning how to breathe again myself.

Curran was living in Washington, but he checked in on me regularly, calling often in those early months. He held space for me in the quiet ways that only a son who is also learning how to be a man can do. There was a tenderness in his tone. He didn't always have the words, but he showed up.

It wasn't until more than a year later that Curran shared something that brought tears to my eyes. He told me how, despite some earlier challenges in their relationship, he could now see how good Skip had been to him. He remembered the drone flights, the basketball games, the quick trips for ice cream where Skip would lean over and whisper, *"Don't tell your mom."* There was fun, laughter, and connection. Even though there were bumps along the way, Curran saw that Skip loved me deeply, and that imprint of love has stayed with him.

Mila, too, saw that love. Whatever issues they may have had between them, she couldn't deny how Skip treated me and that mattered. My kids hadn't witnessed that kind of devotion in their fathers' relationship with me. To see a man hold me, support me, kiss me on the forehead, and call me "his girl" left a healing mark.

What I wish more people understood is that grieving as a parent is like walking through a forest fire while trying to shelter others from the flames. There is no perfect way. Sometimes you get burned. Sometimes you forget the map. Sometimes you realize all you can do is keep going and hope your children feel the love beneath the smoke.

We're still healing together. And that's okay. Healing doesn't follow a straight line. It curves. It spirals. It returns. And so do we, to each other, and to the love that never left.

If you're parenting through grief, here are a few things that might help:

- **Give yourself permission to grieve out loud, but also to take breaks.** Your children don't need you to be perfect. They just need to know you're still here, loving them through the ache.
- **Let them grieve in their own way. Some kids get quiet.** Others get angry. Some distract. Some dive deep. There's no wrong path. Offer support, but don't demand closeness. Trust that distance can be its own kind of coping.

- **Create soft places for connection.** This might look like watching a show together in silence, lighting a candle at dinner, or sharing a memory about your loved one without forcing a response. Ritual and rhythm matter, even if they're simple.

- **Be honest.** It's okay to say, "I'm sad today," or "I miss them too." That kind of transparency models emotional truth and gives your kids permission to feel without shame.

- **Ask for help.** You are not meant to carry this alone. Let others step in, especially for things that feel too heavy right now, such as rides to school, meals, errands, and emotional check-ins.

- **And lastly, keep showing up.** Even if it's messy. Even if you're tired. Even if the only thing you can offer that day is your presence. Presence is enough.

Grief might change the landscape of your family, but love is what will keep you tethered. And love, when tended gently, has the power to rebuild.

CHAPTER 38

SOUL CONTRACT CLARITY

Not every goodbye is a failure. Some are fulfillments. Some exits, no matter how painful, are part of the original agreement our souls made long before this life began. They're not punishments or betrayals. They're turning points that activate the exact growth our soul came here to embody.

If you're reading this after a loss that changed you, you're not alone. Below are some reflection prompts and insights to help you navigate your own soul contract clarity.

What Is a Soul Contract?

A soul contract is an agreement made between souls before we incarnate into human form. These agreements aren't always easy or obvious. They're designed to support our evolution, which can show up in many different ways.

Sometimes a soul agrees to teach us through deep love, while other times the teaching comes through challenge, loss, or contrast. It may be the partner who breaks our heart, the child who forces us to grow, the friend who holds space, or the mentor who triggers a dormant remembering. It might even be the person we perceive as an antagonist, the one who pushes us so hard we're forced to reclaim our power.

These roles are not random. They're chosen with care, and often, with a kind of soul-level love that transcends the pain they may create in this life. Some contracts are brief, perhaps a moment of recognition, a sudden shift, a crossing of paths that changes everything. Others last years or lifetimes, unfolding in layers.

Sometimes, a soul contract ends before we expect. The lesson may be complete. The soul may be ready to evolve in another dimension, continuing their path in a form we can no longer touch. That ending can feel brutal from the human perspective, but from a higher view, it's part of the plan we agreed to long ago.

These contracts are not fixed. They are dynamic. They can be renegotiated, rewritten, and released. No matter how painful, confusing, or chaotic they seem, they are always in service to your expansion. Even when it feels like your world is falling apart, your soul is doing something sacred, intentional, and aligned with what you came here to learn and become.

Reflective Questions

Take your time. There's no rush. Let these unfold as you're ready.

1. What do you feel your soul was learning through this relationship?
It could be about self-worth, boundaries, patience, grief, or radical love.

2. What do you sense their soul was learning through you?
Be honest, even if it's bittersweet. Sometimes we teach by example. Sometimes by contrast.

3. What patterns did this loss break open?

Did it free you from something you didn't realize was holding you back?

4. What are you no longer willing to carry?

This might include outdated roles, survival modes, or stories about who you have to be.

5. What would it look like to live from the clarity this experience gave you?

Let that answer come from your soul rather than your fear.

Signs the Soul Contract Is Complete

You may feel a sudden and surprising peace, even amid ongoing grief. It can come out of nowhere, like a soft wave settling over you after months of storm. Nothing may have changed externally, but something inside you has shifted. You're no longer resisting what happened. You're breathing with it. Even though grief still visits in quiet or messy ways, there's a new steadiness holding you. You have a sense that somehow, on some level, it's okay to keep living.

You may also feel an inner permission slip to move on that is clear, calm, and unforced. It's not the kind of "moving on" people try to rush you into, but a deep, quiet knowing that it's safe to move forward, and that you're allowed to laugh and want again.

You can create a future that doesn't erase the past, but includes it. For the first time, it doesn't feel like a betrayal to be happy. It feels like a continuation of the love that was always there.

There might be a sudden urge to live more fully, more honestly, or more expansively than ever before. Something wakes up in you. It could be the realization that life is short or that time is sacred. You may notice you've been dimming your light in ways that no longer make sense.

It's not about perfection; instead, it's about alignment. You may feel called to speak your truth more clearly, to drop old patterns, and to say yes to things your past self would've avoided. This isn't recklessness. It's remembrance.

Then there are the signs, including visitations, synchronicities, and dreams that feel more real than waking life. You may hear their voice in your heart, feel their presence during a song, see repeating numbers, flickering lights, or perfectly timed symbols that no one else would notice but you.

You may sense that the relationship isn't gone, it's just different. The way they love you hasn't stopped. It's just shifted forms. In those moments, you're reminded that you are not making this up. They are still with you. The connection has evolved, but it hasn't ended.

If You're Still in the Process

Some soul contracts shift but don't end. If you're unsure whether the contract is complete or evolving, sit with these questions:

- Is this dynamic expanding or draining me?
- Does it reflect who I've become or who I used to be?
- What do I need to feel free?

Sometimes, the completion isn't about walking away. It's about rewriting the terms from your highest self.

Closing Ritual (Optional)

If you're ready to mark the end of a contract or shift into a new version of it, you might try this simple ritual:

1. Light a candle. Place a hand on your heart.
2. Speak their name. Thank them for their role, even if it was painful.
3. Say aloud:
   "I honor the soul contract between us. I release what is complete. I carry forward only the love, the growth, and the clarity. I am free. And so are you."
4. Blow out the candle with intention.

This isn't about forgetting. It's about remembering differently from the level of the soul.

CHAPTER 39

YOUR GRIEF IS YOUR GIFT

Grief changed me at a depth I didn't know existed. It wasn't gentle. It wasn't poetic. It was gut-wrenching, wild, and unrelenting. It brought me to my knees and stripped away the parts of me that could no longer survive in my new reality. But in that breaking, space was made. And in that space, something sacred was born.

Grief taught me presence. Not the kind you practice in meditation, but the kind that grabs your face and demands that you look and feel every raw edge of your humanity. It brought me closer to my soul and to the truth of impermanence. It reminded me of the miracle of still being here.

Through that sacred rupture, I became a more powerful channel. My connection to the galactic realms deepened, not despite the grief, but because of it. The veil between worlds thinned, and I learned that love never ends. Death isn't an ending. It's a transformation. Those we love don't leave us. They take off their human costumes and meet us in the frequency of truth.

Grief didn't just expand my heart; it expanded my mission. It helped me embody compassion in a way that no training ever could. It helped me hold space for others' sorrow, for their questions, for their becoming. It gave me the courage to be fully seen, not as someone who "has it all figured out," but as someone who has walked through fire and chosen to rise.

So if you're in the thick of it, please know this: your grief isn't a detour. It's an initiation. While it may feel like a burden, realize it's also a bridge that connects your human experience to your highest expression.

It's okay to take your time. It's okay to not be okay. When you're ready, let your grief become fuel. Let it carve out space for something even greater to move through you.

If you're walking this path, here are a few ways to support yourself as grief shapes and refines you. Some of these will be expanded upon in the next chapter:

- **Name what's true.** Write down what hurts. Say it out loud to someone who can hold it without trying to fix it. Let the grief be witnessed. Not analyzed. Not solved. Just seen.

- **Find a rhythm.** In the chaos, small rituals can become anchors. Light a candle each morning. Take a walk at sunset. Speak their name before bed. These gestures, though simple, create containers for processing what otherwise feels too big.

- **Let your body grieve.** Emotions live in the tissues. Crying, shaking, stretching, and dancing are all valid ways to move grief. You don't need to intellectualize every feeling. Sometimes release comes through movement, not meaning.

- **Welcome the visitations.** If you feel their presence in dreams, in synchronicities, in sudden memories, trust that. The veil is thin when the heart is cracked wide open. You're not imagining things. Love finds a way to stay.

- **Notice what's emerging.** Grief clears. It doesn't just take, it makes space. Pay attention to the nudges, the new ideas, and the surprising strengths. Your soul is speaking. Let the grief be a listening portal, not just a wound.

- **Let support meet you.** Whether it's a therapist, a friend, or your spiritual team, let others help carry the weight. You don't have to do this alone, even if it feels like you are.

Journal Prompts for Integration:

- Where has grief softened me? Where has it strengthened me?
- What parts of my old identity did grief help me shed?
- How has my ability to connect with others on Earth or in higher realms shifted since my loss?
- What new gifts or callings have emerged in the wake of my grief?
- If my grief were a guide, what would it be teaching me right now?
- What part of myself am I reclaiming through this process?

There is no map for this, but your heart knows the way. Let it lead you, gently, slowly, and honestly, back to the part of you that never left. The one that came here to feel it all … and still rise.

CHAPTER 40

MOVING THE ENERGY OF GRIEF

Grief is never just mental or emotional. It's also energetic. It lives in your cells, your breath, your bones, and your frequency. After Skip passed, I realized I couldn't just "think" my way through the pain. I had to move it, transmute it, and honor it as sacred.

Grief doesn't end. It shape-shifts. Some days it's foggy. Other days, a sharp edge. Sometimes it feels strangely quiet, as if you should be feeling more, but you can't. Then out of nowhere, it knocks the wind out of you. Again.

This chapter isn't about "healing" grief. It's about helping it move because when grief stagnates, it turns inward. It becomes numbness, fatigue, or a lingering sense of being untethered. When we allow it to move through the body, through ritual, and through voice, it starts to transmute into clarity, purpose, and eventually, peace.

These are the practices and tools that carried me through the most raw, soul-stripped season of my life. I offer them not as a prescription, but as an invitation. Take what resonates. Leave what doesn't. Let your soul guide your healing.

Below are tools to support that process. Let them meet you where you are.

1. Name What Hurts (And Let It Speak)

Grief isn't just the absence of someone. It's the absence of a thousand somethings, such as their voice, their routines, and the future you thought you were building.

One of the most powerful ways to begin moving through grief is to name it. Not just "I miss them," but:

- "I miss being someone who didn't wake up with a lump in her throat."
- "I miss who I was when I thought we still had time."
- "I miss not having to explain why I'm not 'over it.'"

Try This:

Each morning or evening, ask yourself: *What part of me is grieving today?*

You might get a clear answer: "My inner protector." "My child self." "The part that thought we had more time."

Let it speak. Let it cry. Let it rage or whisper.

Naming gives the grief form. When it has form, it can move.

2. Move the Body, Move the Grief

In the first several weeks after the death, I would dance around my bedroom to Skip's Depeche Mode Pandora station. I would let my body move in whatever way it was called to do. I would also walk the neighborhood to move my body.

Grief isn't just emotional. It's somatic. It lives in the tissue, in the joints, and in the chest cavity. You don't need to understand it to release it. You need to give it motion.

When you move your body, you create space for grief to move too. It doesn't necessarily disappear, but it shape-shifts. Grief likes rhythm, breath, and sway.

Try This:

- Take a walk without your phone. Let your breath and feet set the pace.
- Put on a song that opens your heart and dance without choreography.
- Shake for two minutes. Stand with knees soft, arms loose, and shake hands, feet, and shoulders, all of it. Let your body release what the mind can't articulate.

If you cry, great. If you don't, that's fine too. The release is happening, even if it's quiet.

3. Work with Water

For the first three weeks after Skip's death, my best friend Jen and I went to the beach almost daily. The salt water held me when nothing else could. The sand reminded me that nothing is ever still. It's constantly shifting, softening, and re-forming. Some days, I floated and let the water wash me clean. Other days, I planted my feet in the sand beneath the surf.

Grief belongs to the element of water. When we suppress it, it stagnates, turning into heaviness, fog, or emotional shutdown. Water is a portal. It doesn't judge. It simply flows.

Water rituals are powerful allies in grief work. They don't require belief systems, just presence.

Try This:

- Take a salt bath and cry into the water. Let it receive your pain without needing to fix it.

- Fill a bowl with water, whisper what you're ready to release into it, and then pour it into the earth.
- Write a letter to your loved one, fold it gently, and float it on a river or ocean if that's available. If not, burn the letter and let the steam or smoke carry it.

Let water hold what feels too heavy to carry.

4. Make an Altar (or a Corner)

I chose an area in my bedroom to create an altar to Skip, which remained up for a few months. I included the beautiful Hawaiian flowers that people gave to me at his celebration of life, leis that were gifted for the celebration, a photo of us on our wedding day in Thailand, a copy of our wedding vows, the vase with his ashes, and other gifts people had given to me after his passing.

Grief can feel chaotic. Creating a sacred space gives it containment. This isn't to restrict it, but to honor it. You don't need to be "spiritual" to do this. You need to care enough to make room.

Try This:

Choose a shelf, a nightstand, or a corner of your room. Add:

- A photo of your loved one (or a symbol that represents them)
- A candle
- A stone, shell, feather, or item that brings peace
- A handwritten note, affirmation, or prayer

You can sit here when you want to feel them or when you want to release them. You can cry, light incense, or breathe.

The altar is not dedicated to the past. It's a place to hold love that still exists.

5. Say the Things

Whenever I was called, I would record myself on my phone. I let it all out, no matter how it flowed. It helped me express exactly what I was feeling or knowing in that moment. I also knew I would one day write a book about this experience, and I wanted to capture the real-time emotions and understanding to refer back to.

One of the deepest wounds in grief is the unsaid. It may be the apology you never gave, the truth you never heard, or the love you never fully spoke.

Energy gets stuck in the silence.

Try This:

- Write them a letter. Say it all. The gratitude, the regret, the confusion.
- Read it out loud to their photo, to the stars, to the ocean.
- Burn it. Or keep it tucked in your altar. Let the energy move out of your body and into form.

If you need to say "I forgive you," say it. If you need to say "You hurt me," say it.

Say the things, not because they can't hear you, but because you need to listen to yourself.

6. Channel It Into Something New

When I chose the vase for Skip's ashes, I also chose a pendant to hold some of his ashes, knowing I would create something special with it. The pendant was a Hawaiian-style fishhook. I incorporated it into a small crystal suncatcher, including amazonite and lapis lazuli beads, with a dolphin, which is Skip's spirit animal. I hung it from my rearview mirror for more than a year after his passing. It felt like he was my co-pilot.

In addition to the suncatcher, I knew I would write this book one day. This is part of my service to share what I have learned with others who need guidance.

Grief is pure energy. Once it starts to move, it becomes potential. It doesn't have to become a career, a calling, or a public story. But it can become something, such as a meal, a playlist, a garden, a ritual, a business, or a boundary.

Try This:

- Make something in their honor. A necklace. A journal. A private playlist.
- Turn what they gave you into service: if they taught you gentleness, teach it. If they made people laugh, create space for joy.
- Create a new tradition: a candle lighting, a seasonal offering, a donation, or a gathering of your own design.

The goal isn't to distract yourself. It's to make space for your new shape to emerge.

7. Speak Your Grief Out Loud

In those early days, I had Jen as my sounding board. She was excellent at holding space for me and saying what I needed to say without judgment. I also used my voice memo when she was asleep and after she had returned home to Washington.

Grief isolates, especially when the people around you want to "fix it," "reframe it," or "give it time." Speaking your grief breaks the spell. It rehumanizes you. It reminds your system that you're not the only one feeling this way.

Try This:

- Share with someone who won't try to solve it. Let them witness.
- Join a grief circle or write your story anonymously. Sometimes being heard without feedback is enough.
- If no one is available, speak to the wind. To the ocean. To your guides. To your higher self. The point is expression, not performance.

You don't have to sound wise. You just have to sound real.

8. Cleanse the Space (and the Energy)

After Skip's passing, the courtyard where it happened held a weight in the air. Our friend Frank took care of the physical cleanup. The next day, Jen and Wendy held a sacred cleansing ceremony. They used sage and palo santo. They drummed. They burned. They spoke prayers aloud. They called in peace, clarity, and grace. It wasn't about erasing what happened. It was about shifting the energy.

Try This:

- Burn incense or light a candle.
- Speak aloud the intention of release.
- Open the windows.
- Play high-frequency music or crystal bowls.
- Use your hands or a feather to move energy.

You don't need to be trained. You just need to be present. Grief lives in space, but so does rebirth.

9. Clear the Physical Items

In the weeks that followed, I began clearing out Skip's personal belong-ings. It wasn't easy, but I knew I needed to create space, both energeti-cally and emotionally. I kept the items that held real meaning. I let go of the ones that didn't. Jen helped me sort, donate, and release.

Try This:

- Focus on one small space at a time.
- Ask yourself if the item has a use for you in your life.
- Release what you can, in that moment, knowing it's a process. It doesn't have to be all or nothing.

If you're in this phase of grieving, trust your pacing. There's no "right" time. Let your intuition guide what stays and what goes. Know that releasing an item doesn't mean releasing love. The soul remains. You can't lose that.

10. Transmuting Through Creation

We turned the place of death into a sanctuary of life. Isaiah and I built hydroponic garden beds in the courtyard. We added a roof to the per-gola. We created a tiki bar and called it The Milky Way. The soil became a canvas. We planted herbs, veggies, and leafy greens. We literally grew life from the place where it ended.

This was sacred transmutation, not spiritual bypassing. It was our way of saying: *This pain will not define this space forever.*

Try This:

- Plant a garden.
- Paint.
- Write a poem.

- Create something new from an old item.

Creation is the language of the soul. Let your grief be your paintbrush.

11. Galactic Communication & Healing

As a Galactic Ambassador, I had already been in communication with the Arcturians, Sirians, Mantis, and other Galactic races for years. But after Skip passed, the frequency changed. Their messages came through stronger, not just in words, but in vibrations. They worked on my physical and energetic body at night, so I could heal faster.

My Galactic Team reminded me: *Souls don't die. Only the form changes.* I channeled light codes. I sat in meditation with galactic frequencies. I asked my team to help me hold my heart when I couldn't hold it myself.

I also reached out to other holistic and energy healers to help me move the energy that was stuck. I got massages. I knew the extra support would amplify my energetic healing.

Try This:

- Sit in stillness.
- Breathe.
- Call in your guides and ask for healing.
- Ask your deceased loved one to show you signs they are there.
- Get a massage.
- Get an energy healing session.

You are never alone.

12. Let Joy Return Without Guilt

I don't remember precisely when moments of joy started showing up again. It was likely on the trip to Washington for Christmas in 2023.

My mom had flown my daughter and me out, as she knew it would likely be her last Christmas. She, my kids, and I spent that holiday with Jen and her family. We baked cookies and played games. We laughed a lot.

The day after returning home, I met Isaiah, who has brought a lot of joy into my life over the last year and a half, no matter what our dating status has been. I have new friends on the island who meet me at my higher frequency, helping me maintain that joyful state.

At some point, joy will start to slip back in. A breeze will feel sweet. A song will make you smile. A moment will feel surprisingly light. Let it. Joy doesn't mean you've "moved on." It means grief has moved through.

Try This:

- Track the micro-joys. A sunset. A joke. A moment of peace. Let them register in your nervous system.
- When guilt rises, say: *I carry them in my joy too.*
- Do something they would've loved, and smile with them, not just for them.

You are allowed to laugh again. To feel whole. To be changed, but still joyful.

13. Choosing to Live

This is the most sacred ritual of all. Choose to keep going. Booking the trips to Egypt and Bali was my declaration. I wouldn't have gone to Egypt if Skip were still alive. He would've been too worried about money. But after his passing, I heard the message clearly: *Take the trip. Live. Don't shrink.*

Every day I woke up and said, "I choose life. I choose healing. I choose expansion." Some days, I said it with conviction. Some days I whispered it through tears, but I said it anyway.

I invite you to do the same. Even when it hurts. Especially when it hurts.

Grief is not a linear process. It's a spiral, a wave, and a sacred unraveling. But with intention, it becomes more than mere survival. It becomes a portal to remembrance, to rebirth, and to a new expression of your soul.

These are the tools and rituals that helped me return to myself. I hope, in your own way, they help you return to yourself. Grief may never entirely leave, but it doesn't have to define your future. Let it shape you. Then let it soften. You are not broken. You are becoming.

CHAPTER 41

THE ENERGY OF THE HOUSE

Homes hold energy. They hold memory in the walls, in the land, in the items we keep and the ones we release. They record joy and trauma alike, sometimes whispering, sometimes screaming. When a traumatic event takes place inside (or outside) a home, that energy lingers until we move it.

After Skip's passing, I knew I couldn't just live in the same space without shifting its energy. I had to reclaim it, not only physically, but energetically, so the home could become a sanctuary once again.

That process began slowly, first, with the practical. We emptied the garage of the massive treadmill, BMW project car, and motorcycle. The garage became a clean slate, soon transforming into Isaiah's glass shop, where artistry, light, and fire now dance.

Then came the fresh paint on the exterior of the house and the roof repairs. There was the daily tending of the courtyard, with new plants and construction. We built raised garden beds in the backyard, supplementing the hydroponic tables we had already created in the very space where Skip had taken his life. What had once held death now blossomed with life. Green shoots. Healing herbs. There was sacred intention in every seed.

I regularly saged the home, inside and out, making sure to clear the courtyard, the garage, and the bedrooms. The smoke acts as a purifier to clear away energy. It wasn't just a ritual. It was survival. It was a reclamation.

Then, something powerful happened. After all the clearing and renewal, I hosted my first group retreat at the house. These men and women walked into my space and didn't sense heaviness. They felt light. They loved the courtyard. They loved the energy. The house felt like a temple. That retreat was confirmation that the frequency had shifted.

In a recent mediumship session, Skip came through with a final affirmation. He called it "The Healing House." It isn't just a home or a shelter. It's a frequency field that supports transformation, transmutation, and spiritual awakening. This home was built on love. Through grief, it has become a container of healing for others.

Rituals for Reclaiming the Energy of Your Space

If you are living in a home that holds grief, trauma, or dense energy, know that you're not powerless. Just as you clear your body and mind, you can clear your space. Here are some suggestions to help you transmute the energy of your home into a sanctuary:

Physical Clearing

- **Declutter and Donate:** Release what no longer serves. Energy can stagnate in old objects, clothes, or furniture connected to painful memories. Letting go makes space for healing.
- **Repair and Refresh:** Fix broken items, paint walls, and deep-clean neglected corners. This is sacred labor—tending to your environment with intention.

Energetic Cleansing

- **Smoke Cleansing (Sage, Palo Santo, or Mugwort):** Move through your home with the smoke, paying particular attention to corners, mirrors, windows, and entryways. Speak a prayer or intention as you go: *"I release what is not mine to carry. I invite in light, peace, and love."*
- **Sound Clearing:** Use singing bowls, clapping, bells, drums, or chanting to shift the frequency of a space. Sound disrupts stagnant energy and calls in higher vibrations.

Anchoring Light

- **Create a Sacred Corner:** Designate a space with crystals, plants, candles, or meaningful objects. Let it be a visual reminder of your healing.
- **Build a Garden (or Indoor Plant Ritual):** If you can't plant outside, nurture life indoors with herbs or flowers. Speak intentions into the soil as you plant. Water with love.

Elemental Support

- **No Beach Nearby? Try a Salt Bath:** Soak in sea salt or Epsom salts to detoxify both your body and mind. Visualize the water drawing grief out and replacing it with light.
- **Daily Clearing Spray:** Mix purified water, a few drops of essential oils (like lavender, rosemary, or frankincense), and a pinch of sea salt in a spray bottle. Mist around your space with a clearing intention.

Express and Release

- **Journaling or Voice Memos:** When emotion floods in, don't bottle it. Write it. Speak it. Let your voice become the container for release. Even 60 seconds of honest expression can move energy that's been stuck for years.

Invite the New

- **Name Your Space:** Like Skip calling our home *The Healing House,* giving your space a sacred name can anchor a new identity and purpose into it.
- **Speak Gratitude to the Walls:** "Thank you for holding me." "Thank you for letting me grieve and heal here." Love changes the blueprint of a place.

You are the priestess or steward of your space. Your grief doesn't just mark an ending. It initiates a transformation.

CHAPTER 42

SUPPORTING SOMEONE IN GRIEF

If you're wondering how to support someone in grief, please know it isn't something to fix. It's not a problem that needs solving or a state to be hurried through. Grief is sacred. It's messy, nonlinear, and deeply personal.

When someone you love is grieving, your presence, not your perfection, is what they will remember. From the heart of someone who's walked through profound loss, here's what truly helped, and what didn't.

What Helped

Being There, Quietly and Consistently

The people who showed up without needing to fix, explain, or fill the silence were my lifelines. They didn't demand answers or try to make the pain go away. They understood that grief isn't something to solve; it's something to be witnessed. A simple message with no expectation of a reply, a warm meal left at my door, a quiet cup of coffee shared in stillness. These small gestures meant everything.

There is a particular comfort in those who can sit with you in the rawness, who don't flinch at the mess of it all, and who don't try to rush you into being "better." Their presence said more than words ever could.

They reminded me that I wasn't alone, even when speaking felt impossible. Sometimes it's not grand acts of support that carry you, but the quiet, steady ones. These people show up, again and again, without needing anything in return.

Offering Practical, Tangible Support

In the early days of grief, even the most minor tasks felt impossible. I could barely think straight, let alone plan meals or handle logistics. What helped most wasn't abstract offers. It was the people who stepped in without waiting for direction. A friend set up a meal train. Others dropped off groceries without fanfare. Some did my yard work.

It wasn't the well-meaning "Let me know if you need anything" that made the difference because, truthfully, I didn't always know what I needed. Even when I did, I didn't always have the energy to reach out and ask. The support that mattered most came from those who didn't need permission to show up. They saw what was required and acted.

These were the gestures that grounded me, the ones that said, "You don't have to hold this all alone." They helped create a sense of structure when everything else had fallen apart. They reminded me that love isn't always loud or emotional. Sometimes it shows up in a casserole, a cleaned-up kitchen, or a quick text saying, "I took care of this for you." That kind of support lives in the body. It eases the nervous system. It creates space to breathe.

Giving Space and Permission to Feel It All

There were days I couldn't answer the phone, respond to texts, hold a conversation, or pretend to be okay. Grief doesn't follow a schedule, and it doesn't always come in predictable waves. Sometimes it flattens you out of nowhere. What helped most were the people who understood that, and who didn't take my silence personally.

They gave me space without disappearing. They didn't push. They didn't need updates or check-ins to validate their support. They held the door open for me when I was ready.

Sometimes that looked like a message with no strings attached. Sometimes it looked like someone dropping something off quietly, or just letting me know they were thinking of me without expecting a response.

What they offered was permission to grieve in the way I needed to. Permission to say no, to cancel plans, to not reply, and to go inward. They didn't need me to be okay to stay close. And that kind of presence that's steady, soft, and unthreatened by distance was healing in its own way.

Remembering with Me

What meant the most were the people who didn't shy away from saying Skip's name. They didn't tiptoe around his memory or act like bringing him up would somehow hurt me more. Instead, they brought him into the room through stories, memories, photos, or even just a simple, "I thought about him today."

Sometimes it was a moment they remembered from years ago. At other times it was a song, a dream, or something small that made them feel his presence. Those moments grounded me. They reminded me that his life didn't disappear just because he wasn't physically here anymore.

When someone you love dies, there's this quiet fear that the world will move on without them. That people will forget. But the ones who remembered with me, who honored his presence without awkwardness or discomfort, gave me such a gift. They allowed the love we shared to keep living, instead of being sealed away in the past. It told me I didn't have to erase him to heal. I could carry him with me, talk about him, laugh about him, and still move forward. Remembering together made the grief lighter. Not gone, but shared. And that made all the difference.

Respecting My Spiritual Path

Not everyone understood the galactic experiences I was having or the signs that came through after Skip passed. Messages in dreams, synchronicities, energy shifts, or the deep knowing I felt in my body, these weren't things I could easily explain. I didn't need everyone to believe in them. What I needed was space to process grief in the multidimensional way it was unfolding for me. This wasn't just about loss. It was about contact, remembrance, soul contracts, and timelines. My path was never going to look traditional, and that's precisely what made it honest.

The people who respected that, who didn't roll their eyes, question my reality, or try to tether me back to something more "acceptable," gave me a freedom that was essential to my healing. Even if they didn't relate, they didn't dismiss it. They listened. They stayed open. That kind of respect meant everything. It allowed me to stay connected to my truth. It allowed me to move through grief in a way that honored both my humanity and my cosmic knowing, and to emerge not just surviving, but more fully myself.

What Didn't Help

Projecting Their Grief Onto Me

When people said things like, "This is going to suck for a long time," or "You're probably going to have to sell the house," it didn't resonate with me. It felt like they were projecting their own fear onto my experience. It was like they couldn't imagine a version of grief that didn't include total devastation.

But I knew, even in the early days, that I wasn't going to stay in that place forever. I knew I was going to be okay. Not because I was bypassing the pain, but because I could feel something steady inside me, something larger holding me through it. I didn't need pity. I needed people to trust that I could walk through it without losing myself. Sometimes the most honest and supportive words are: "I'm so sorry. I'm here with you."

Some people looked at me, going to business networking meetings, getting out of the house, functioning, and assumed I wasn't really processing my emotions. It was as if the only valid expression of grief was being a sobbing mess, unable to leave my bed.

Others approached me with tears in their own eyes, hugging me as if I were about to collapse, thinking that's what I needed. But what they were really doing was projecting how they imagined they would feel onto me. My grief didn't look like theirs. That didn't mean it was any less real. I was feeling everything. I was also allowing myself to keep living. The kindest thing anyone could've done was trust me to know what I needed, and honor that my process didn't have to mirror theirs.

Probing for Details

One of the most painful parts in the aftermath wasn't just the loss. It was how people approached it. Some asked questions I wasn't prepared to answer: how he died, whether there was a note, what I thought I could've done differently, if I knew what his mind-state was at the time. These weren't curious strangers. These were people who meant well, but didn't realize how invasive those questions could feel.

Unless someone explicitly invites you into that level of intimacy, don't ask. Let the grieving person guide what they're ready to share, and when. Even if you think you need to know to understand or support them, you don't. You don't need the details to offer compassion.

Sometimes the most respectful thing you can do is sit with someone in silence, or say, "I'm here if you ever want to talk, but I won't push." Pushing, even gently, can retraumatize someone who's still trying to put the pieces back together. Not all parts of a story are meant to be spoken aloud. Some are intended to be held sacred.

Centering Themselves

There were moments when I'd be raw, barely holding myself together, and someone would step in, not to hold space, but to make it about them. They'd launch into their own grief story or share a long-winded spiritual philosophy about death, karma, or soul contracts without actually tuning in to where I was or what I needed in that moment.

While I know that shared experiences can be powerful and healing, timing and intention matter. If the story is being told to comfort the speaker more than the person grieving, it stops being a connection. It becomes emotional hijacking.

Grief isn't an invitation for someone else to process their pain through you. It's not the time to prove how much you understand or to offer a performance of empathy. The best support often comes from presence, not stories, theories, or solutions. Just be there for them, quietly and sincerely, without making it about anything else.

If you're going to share, ask yourself: Is this for them, or is this for me? If you're not sure, it's okay to say, "I'm here with you," and leave space for whatever needs to arise.

Imposing Timelines

While I didn't personally experience people telling me I was grieving too long, I know many do. Phrases like "Aren't you better yet?" or "It's time to move on" can land like daggers. They often come from discomfort, or someone else's need to tidy up what can't be made neat.

But grief doesn't follow a schedule. There's no universal marker for when someone should feel "healed," and trying to force one only adds pressure and shame to a process that's already heavy enough.

In my case, I actually experienced the opposite. When I began a new relationship with Isaiah, some people felt I was moving too fast. They didn't see all the layers underneath, such as the spiritual connection and the past/parallel-life remembrance.

The timing didn't make logical sense to outsiders, but it made soul sense to me. From the outside, it may have looked like bypassing, but from the inside, it was part of my integration. I wasn't escaping the grief. I was expanding inside it.

As I've mentioned several times, grief isn't linear. It doesn't unfold the same way for everyone, and healing doesn't mean staying still. Sometimes it means building something new. Sometimes it means sitting quietly for a long time. The kindest thing we can do is stop measuring each other's timelines and start trusting that the soul knows what it's doing, even when the path looks different from what we expected.

Assuming I Should Stay Married to the Dead

Skip's passing marked the end of that marriage in this human life. And yet, some people treated it like the bond should remain untouched forever, like dating again was a kind of betrayal, as if I were cheating on someone who was no longer physically here.

There was an unspoken expectation with some people that I should hold a permanent place at his side, even after death. I should stay emotionally tethered, romantically unavailable, indefinitely loyal in a way that denied my own aliveness.

But the truth is, Skip's death didn't just leave a space beside me; it invited me into a new chapter. And he knew that. He gave me permission, from the other side, to keep living and loving. To move forward, not away from him, but with the part of him that still lives inside me.

I wasn't rushing. I wasn't escaping. I was listening to my soul's timing. The assumption that I was "moving on too soon" said more about others' discomfort with death, love, and change than it did about me.

Grief and devotion can coexist with desire for a new beginning. What ended was the form of our marriage, not the love, the lessons, or the honoring of what we shared. Choosing to open my heart again was not abandonment. It was evolution.

If You're Not Sure What to Say

Here are some words that helped me the most:

"I don't know what to say, but I'm here."

"This is so hard, and I love you."

"Would you like me to check in later this week, or would you prefer space?"

"I can't take the pain away, but I want to walk beside you."

It doesn't need to be perfect. Just be real. Let your love speak more than your logic.

Grief reveals who is willing to sit with the unknown. It clarifies relationships and shows you who can hold the silence, the chaos, and the unanswerable. If you are someone trying to support a grieving friend or family member, thank you. Even your desire to do it well means more than you know. Your quiet presence may be the very thing that keeps them breathing when the world has gone dark.

CHAPTER 43

WHAT REMAINS AFTER THE FIRE

If you've made it to these final pages, thank you. Truly. This wasn't just my story. It was a reflection of so many of ours—the grief, the unraveling, and the moments of grace that arrived in the wreckage.

Maybe you've walked through your own loss. Perhaps you're standing at a threshold now, unsure what comes next. Maybe you're just beginning to remember who you are.

Wherever you are, I hope these words have reminded you that you're not alone in it. There's no map for this kind of journey, but there are markers with love, presence, and truth. Even in devastation, life leaves us a shimmer to follow. A whisper. A thread. And in the quiet space between what was and what's next, something new begins.

When Skip died, everything I knew rearranged. But over time, through the ache and the unexpected beauty that followed, I came to see it wasn't just an ending. It was a soul contract unfolding. A passage into deeper embodiment. It was one I didn't plan for, but was always meant to walk.

This book was never about resolution. It's about what remains. The quiet truth. The hard-earned wisdom. The deeper love. It's about how grief reshapes us, and how, if we let it, it also refines us.

So I leave you with this:

What part of you is rising now?

What truth is knocking on your heart?

What chapter of your soul story are you living, and are you willing to meet it fully?

There's no rush. There's no finish line. There's only the invitation to keep going, to keep breathing, to let the next version of you arrive.

I'm still walking, healing, and listening. And I'll say what I most needed to hear: You are not broken. You are becoming.

We came here to love. To lose. To remember. And to rise.

And we were never meant to do it alone.

With love in the remembering,

Dr. Lisa

"It's possible to go on, no matter how impossible it seems, and that in time, the grief ... lessens. It may not go away completely, but after a while, it's not so overwhelming."

–Nicholas Sparks

ABOUT THE AUTHOR

Dr. Lisa Thompson is a globally recognized leader in multidimensional awakening who has helped thousands of individuals activate their highest potential and step into their soul-aligned purpose. She is a best-selling author, speaker, and founder of the Infinity Healing Method™—an energy healing certification for healers.

As a Galactic Ambassador and multidimensional channeler, Dr. Lisa communicates with 13 higher-dimensional ET races—primarily the Arcturian Uluru—bringing through transformative galactic wisdom and healing frequencies to support humanity's ascension.

A lifelong experiencer of extraterrestrial contact, she serves as a guide for those ready to awaken their soul's highest calling, shift timelines consciously, and fully embody 5D consciousness. Her teachings help you clear energetic blocks, release limitations, and unlock more of your unique spiritual gifts, so you can live with greater clarity, purpose, and power.

With a PhD in Evolutionary Biology from the University of Chicago, Dr. Lisa merges cutting-edge science with multidimensional spirituality, making her a pioneering voice in the global awakening movement.

Working with Dr. Lisa means stepping into a higher vibration, mastering your energy, and aligning with your highest timeline. Through her courses, activations, and energy healing techniques, you will:

- Expand your consciousness and access deeper levels of wisdom
- Release subconscious blocks that hold you back from your true potential
- Activate your intuitive and multidimensional abilities
- Shift into a reality of joy, abundance, and flow

The Love That Remains

May these pages remind you that love never ends. To continue feeling the presence of your loved one, receive your free gift, *The Love That Remains: Simple Practices to Stay Connected to Your Loved Ones.*

Inside, you'll find: a guide to recognizing the signs your loved one is reaching out, practices to prepare your vibration for connection, simple ways to receive and trust those signs, and a meditative journey to help you experience the love that still surrounds you.

Claim your gift:
TheLoveThatRemains.com

Stay Connected with Dr. Lisa

You can connect with Lisa online and via social media here:

Websites:

DrLisaJThompson.com

BigIslandUFOTours.com

Facebook:

facebook.com/DrLisaThompsonAuthor

facebook.com/BigIslandUFOTours

Instagram:

instagram.com/galactic_drlisathompson/